Introduction:

Introduction of Book	2
Block of the Month Breakdown	3
Vintage Quilt Fabric Requirements	4
Vintage Quilt Reference Photo	5
Modern Quilt Fabric Requirements	6
Modern Quilt Reference Photo	7

Quilt Blocks:

Album Block	8		Hidden Star Block	32
Bear's Track Block	10		Log Cabin Block	34
Birds in the Air Block	12		Maple Star Block	36
Buzzard's Roost Block	14		Memory Block	38
Capital T Block	16		Nonsense Block	40
Checkerboard Block	18		Patchwork Big O Block	42
Churn Dash Block	20		Pinwheel Geese Block	44
Crown of Thorns Block	22		Rocky Mountain Puzzle Block	46
Darting Birds Block	24		Southern Star Block	48
Fool's Puzzle Block	26		Split Nine Patch Block	50
Four X's Block	28		Twin Star Block	52
Friendship Star Block	30		Weathervane Block	54

Framed Blocks:

Framed Blocks Cheat Sheet	56
Small Corner Triangle Framed Block	58
Small Half Square Triangle Framed Block	60
Small Patchwork Framed Block	62
Small Three Geese Framed Block	64
Medium Background Framed Block	66
Large Background Framed Block	68

Finishing:

Summer Moon Quilt Finishing	70

Summer Moon Book by Carrie Nelson

Introduction OF BOOK

The Summer Moon Story

Sharing the story or history of a quilt is often the hardest part of writing a book. Sometimes quilts are just meant to be. While I did not have a clear, specific plan in mind when I started making this quilt, Summer Moon turned out exactly how I pictured it before I started. Pure kismet.

I envisioned blocks in multiple sizes with a setting that wouldn't line up evenly and wouldn't have a lot of negative space. It was fun, but also a risk. Since I didn't have a set plan to sew by, I didn't know if it would work until my blocks were finished.

The Summer Moon quilt is for my fellow quilters who love gorgeous samplers packed with crisp blocks, but also crave a touch of whimsy. While you'll have a specific plan in mind when you make your quilt, I hope you'll enjoy the process as much as I did.

Blocks, Frames and Fabric

This book includes instructions for 24 quilt blocks that are made once in the Small, Medium and Large sizes for a total of 72 blocks. The blocks measure 5", 6 ½" and 8" unfinished. The sizes sound odd, but I promise you it all works!

There are different framing options for the blocks which serve two purposes. They make the blocks the same finished size and allow them to float. The Small Blocks have four setting options, and the Medium and Large Blocks have one setting option each. To make the Summer Moon Quilt exactly as pictured, follow the Framed Blocks Cheat Sheet on page 57.

We have also shown the quilt in two colorways to help you expand your possibilities. The fabric requirements to make the entire quilt are found on pages 4 and 6. If you would like to make the blocks individually, the fabric requirements are listed within the blocks instructions

The Scrap Factor

Using scrappy backgrounds isn't for everyone. It's all about the look you want for your finished quilt. A single background tends to give the blocks greater prominence, while scrappy backgrounds soften the overall look.

When it comes to pairing backgrounds with prints, I try to vary the scale and print. For example: a large print with a smaller print, dots with stripes, florals with geometrics, etc. Some blocks will have high contrast, some will be a little bit muddled. But that's the look I like.

As you pair different fabrics, you'll figure out your preferences pretty quickly. But wait until all the blocks are done before you re-make anything... you might be surprised how it all comes together when the blocks are assembled.

Pre-Carrie-ous Tips: Before You Start

There are a few things I want to share about making these blocks.

1. As cute as they are, small blocks can be a challenge to piece. We recommend having an accurate ¼" seam, setting your seams and using a shorter stitch length.

2. Cut and piece all three sizes at the same time? Or one by one? Whatever makes the most sense to you is the best method, especially if it keeps the seam ripper in the drawer. I liked making them at the same time, because the process was the same and that kept me organized. Whichever process you choose, I recommend using design boards to keep your pieces together.

3. To cut your fabric most efficiently, cut the Large Block first, Medium Block second and Small Block last.

I hope that Summer Moon sparks your imagination, challenges you to try new blocks, and above all else, lets you enjoy the whole creative process.

Summer Moon Book by Carrie Nelson

Block of the Month
BREAKDOWN

MONTH 1	Album Block Page 8	Churn Dash Block Page 20	Fool's Puzzle Block Page 26	
MONTH 2	Capital T Block Page 16	Hidden Star Block Page 32	Pinwheel Geese Block Page 44	
MONTH 3	Bear's Track Block Page 10	Buzzard's Roost Block Page 14	Crown of Thorns Block Page 22	
MONTH 4	Birds in the Air Block Page 12	Split Nine Patch Block Page 50	Twin Star Block Page 52	
MONTH 5	Maple Star Block Page 36	Patchwork Big O Block Page 42	Southern Star Block Page 48	
MONTH 6	Checkerboard Block Page 18	Darting Birds Block Page 24	Nonsense Block Page 40	
MONTH 7	Four X's Block Page 28	Log Cabin Block Page 34	Memory Block Page 38	
MONTH 8	Friendship Star Block Page 30	Rocky Mountain Puzzle Block Page 46	Weathervane Block Page 54	
MONTH 9	Small Corner Triangle Framed Block Page 58	Small Half Square Triangle Framed Block Page 60	Small Patchwork Framed Block Page 62	Small Three Geese Framed Block Page 64
MONTH 10	Medium Background Framed Block Page 66	Large Background Framed Block Page 68	Finishing Page 70	

Summer Moon Book by Carrie Nelson

Vintage Quilt
FABRIC REQUIREMENTS

List includes fabric requirements to make the entire quilt if you want to sew as a quilt kit.
Fabric requirements for each block are listed on the individual block pages if you want to sew as a block of the month.

Fabric	Use	Amount
5080-12	Blocks	½ yard
5080-13	Blocks	½ yard
5080-15	Blocks	⅝ yard
5080-18	Blocks	¾ yard
5081-13	Blocks	⅜ yard
5081-15	Blocks	⅝ yard
5081-16	Blocks	¾ yard
5081-17	Blocks	⅝ yard
5082-11	Blocks	½ yard
5083-12	Blocks	¾ yard
5083-18	Blocks	½ yard
5084-13	Blocks	⅝ yard
5084-15	Blocks	½ yard
5085-12	Blocks	⅝ yard
5085-15	Blocks	½ yard
5085-16	Blocks	⅝ yard
5085-17	Blocks	½ yard
5085-18	Blocks	⅜ yard
5085-11	Background & Border	2 yards
1580-11	Background	1 ¼ yards
1580-12	Background	1 yard
1584-11	Background	1 ⅜ yards
1588-13	Background	1 ⅓ yards
8654-59	Background	1 ⅜ yards
17966-20	Background	1 yard
29067-31	Background	1 ⅛ yards
5086-15	Binding	⅞ yard
5080-11	Backing	5 yards

The Vintage Quilt features fabric from the following Moda Fabrics collections: Lollipop Garden by Lella Boutique, Essential Dots, Later Alligator by Sandy Gervais, Modern Backgrounds Paper by Zen Chic and Strawberry Jam by Corey Yoder.

Summer Moon Book by Carrie Nelson

Vintage Quilt
REFERENCE PHOTO

Finished size: 70 ½" x 78 ¾"

Summer Moon Book by Carrie Nelson

Modern Quilt
FABRIC REQUIREMENTS

List includes fabric requirements to make the entire quilt if you want to sew as a quilt kit.
Fabric requirements for each block are listed on the individual block pages if you want to sew as a block of the month.

Fabric	Use	Amount
1680-15M	Blocks	½ yard
1680-16M	Blocks	½ yard
1680-18M	Blocks	½ yard
1681-16M	Blocks	⅝ yard
1681-17M	Blocks	½ yard
1682-22M	Blocks	½ yard
1683-15M	Blocks	¾ yard
1683-16M	Blocks	½ yard
1683-17M	Blocks	½ yard
1684-16M	Blocks	½ yard
1684-18M	Blocks	⅝ yard
1685-15	Blocks	⅔ yard
1686-14	Blocks	⅝ yard
1686-16	Blocks	½ yard
1686-17	Blocks	½ yard
1660-20	Blocks	½ yard
1660-21	Blocks	⅝ yard
30150-63	Blocks	⅔ yard
1684-11M	Background	1 ⅓ yards
1685-11	Background & Border	2 yards
1580-12	Background	1 ⅜ yards
1584-11	Background	1 yard
1671-22	Background	1 yard
1674-18	Background	1 ¼ yards
1675-13	Background	1 ⅜ yards
30150-101	Background	1 ⅛ yards
1682-22M	Binding	⅞ yard
1681-11M	Backing	5 yards

The Modern Quilt features fabric from the following Moda Fabrics collections: Day in Paris by Zen Chic, Grunge Basics by BasicGrey, Modern Backgrounds Paper by Zen Chic, Modern Backgrounds More Paper by Zen Chic and Spotted by Zen Chic.

Summer Moon Book by Carrie Nelson

Modern Quilt
REFERENCE PHOTO

Finished size: 70 ½" x 78 ¾"

Summer Moon Book by Carrie Nelson

Album BLOCK

Make 1 Small Block 5" square unfinished
Make 1 Medium Block 6 ½" square unfinished
Make 1 Large Block 8" square unfinished

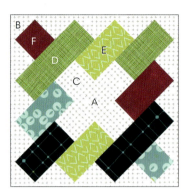

Make 1 Small Block 5" square unfinished
Make 1 Medium Block 6 ½" square unfinished
Make 1 Large Block 8" square unfinished

Vintage Fabric Requirements:

8654-59　　　5080-13　　　5081-17　　　5083-12
Fabrics A to C　Fabrics D to F　Fabrics D to F　Fabrics D to F
⅜ yard　　　10" x 15"　　　10" x 15"　　　10" x 15"

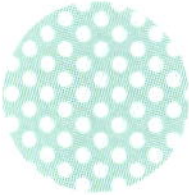

5085-15　　　5085-16
Fabrics D to F　Fabrics D to F
10" x 15"　　　10" x 15"

Modern Fabric Requirements:

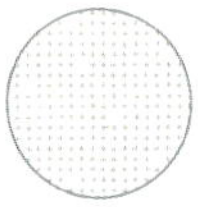

1675-13　　　1682-22M　　　1683-17M　　　1685-15
Fabrics A to C　Fabrics D to F　Fabrics D to F　Fabrics D to F
⅜ yard　　　10" x 15"　　　10" x 15"　　　10" x 15"

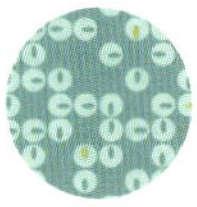

1686-14　　　30150-63
Fabrics D to F　Fabrics D to F
10" x 15"　　　10" x 15"

Cutting Instructions:

		Small Block	Medium Block	Large Block
Background	A	1 - 1 ¼" x 2 ¾" rectangle	1 - 1 ½" x 3 ½" rectangle	1 - 1 ¾" x 4 ¼" rectangle
	B	16 - 1 ¼" x 2" rectangles	16 - 1 ½" x 2 ½" rectangles	16 - 1 ¾" x 2 ¾" rectangles
	C	2 - 1 ¼" squares	2 - 1 ½" squares	2 - 1 ¾" squares
Album	D	1 - 1 ¼" x 2 ¾" rectangle (from each)	1 - 1 ½" x 3 ½" rectangle (from each)	1 - 1 ¾" x 4 ¼" rectangle (from each)
	E	2 - 1 ¼" x 2" rectangles (from each)	2 - 1 ½" x 2 ½" rectangles (from each)	2 - 1 ¾" x 3" rectangles (from each)
	F	1 - 1 ¼" square (from each)	1 - 1 ½" square (from each)	1 - 1 ¾" square (from each)

Summer Moon Book by Carrie Nelson

Album BLOCK

Piecing Instructions:

Fabric placement is intended to be scrappy.

Assemble Partial Album Unit matching centers.

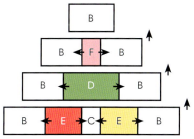 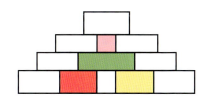

Make two for each Block.

Assemble Album Unit matching centers.

You will not use all Fabric D rectangles, Fabric E rectangles and Fabric F squares.

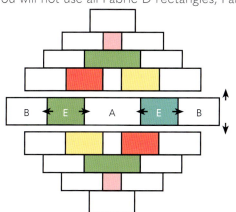 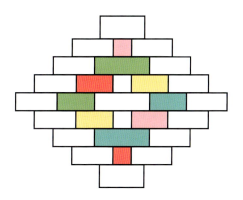

Make one for each Block.

TRIM Album Block to measure:

Small	5" square
Medium	6 ½" square
Large	8" square

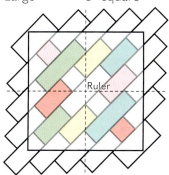 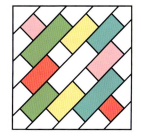

Make one Small Block.
Make one Medium Block.
Make one Large Block.

Summer Moon Book by Carrie Nelson

Bear's Track
BLOCK

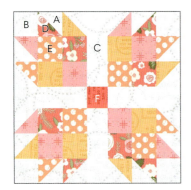

Make 1 Small Block — 5" square unfinished
Make 1 Medium Block — 6 ½" square unfinished
Make 1 Large Block — 8" square unfinished

Make 1 Small Block — 5" square unfinished
Make 1 Medium Block — 6 ½" square unfinished
Make 1 Large Block — 8" square unfinished

Vintage Fabric Requirements:

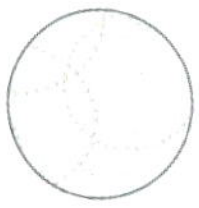

1584-11 — Fabrics A to C — Fat Quarter
5080-13 — Fabrics D & E — 10" x 15" 
5081-17 — Fabrics D & E — 10" x 15"
5083-12 — Fabrics D & E — 10" x 15" 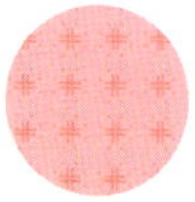

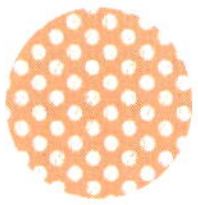

5085-18 — Fabrics D & E — 10" x 15"
5081-13 — Fabric F — 10" square

Modern Fabric Requirements:

1580-12 — Fabrics A to C — Fat Quarter
1683-17M — Fabrics D & E — 10" x 15" 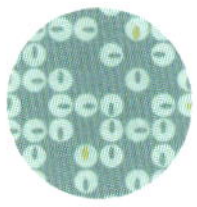
1684-18M — Fabrics D & E — 10" x 15" 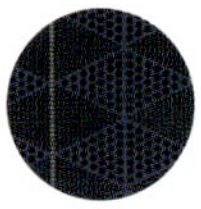
1686-14 — Fabrics D & E — 10" x 15" 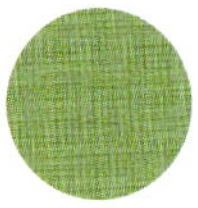

30150-63 — Fabrics D & E — 10" x 15"
1685-15 — Fabric F — 10" square 

Cutting Instructions:

		Small Block	Medium Block	Large Block
Background	A	8 - 1 ½" squares	8 - 1 ¾" squares	8 - 2" squares
	B	4 - 1 ⅛" squares	4 - 1 ⅜" squares	4 - 1 ⅝" squares
	C	4 - 1 ¼" x 2 ⅜" rectangles	4 - 1 ¼" x 3 ⅛" rectangles	4 - 1 ¼" x 3 ⅞" rectangles
Bear's Track	D	2 - 1 ½" squares (from each)	2 - 1 ¾" squares (from each)	2 - 2" squares (from each)
	E	4 - 1 ⅛" squares (from each)	4 - 1 ⅜" squares (from each)	4 - 1 ⅝" squares (from each)
Center	F	1 - 1 ¼" square	1 - 1 ¼" square	1 - 1 ¼" square

Summer Moon Book by Carrie Nelson

Bear's Track BLOCK

Piecing Instructions:

Fabric placement is intended to be scrappy.

• •

Draw a diagonal line on the wrong side of the Fabric A squares.

With right sides facing, layer a Fabric A square with a Fabric D square.

Stitch ¼" from each side of the drawn line.

Cut apart on the marked line.

Half Square Triangle Unit should measure:

Small	1 ⅛" square
Medium	1 ⅜" square
Large	1 ⅝" square

Make sixteen for each Block.

• •

Assemble Unit.

Bear's Track Unit should measure:

Small	2 ⅜" square
Medium	3 ⅛" square
Large	3 ⅞" square

Make four for each Block.

Assemble Block.

Bear's Track Block should measure:

Small	5" square
Medium	6 ½" square
Large	8" square

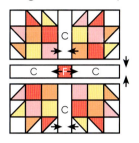 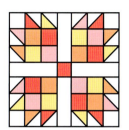

Make one Small Block.
Make one Medium Block.
Make one Large Block.

Summer Moon Book by Carrie Nelson

Birds in the Air
BLOCK

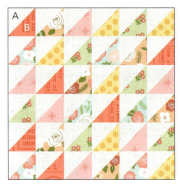

Make 1 Small Block — 5" square unfinished
Make 1 Medium Block — 6 ½" square unfinished
Make 1 Large Block — 8" square unfinished

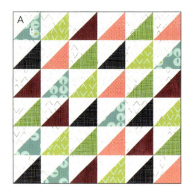

Make 1 Small Block — 5" square unfinished
Make 1 Medium Block — 6 ½" square unfinished
Make 1 Large Block — 8" square unfinished

Vintage Fabric Requirements:

1580-11
Fabric A
⅓ yard

5080-15
Fabric B
10" x 15"

5080-18
Fabric B
10" x 15"

5081-13
Fabric B
10" x 15"

5082-11
Fabric B
10" x 15"

5083-12
Fabric B
10" x 15"

5085-17
Fabric B
10" x 15"

Modern Fabric Requirements:

1685-11
Fabric A
⅓ yard

1682-22M
Fabric B
10" x 15"

1683-17M
Fabric B
10" x 15"

1685-15
Fabric B
10" x 15"

1686-14
Fabric B
10" x 15"

1660-21
Fabric B
10" x 15"

30150-63
Fabric B
10" x 15"

Cutting Instructions:

		Small Block	Medium Block	Large Block
Background	A	18 - 1 ⅝" squares	18 - 1 ⅞" squares	18 - 2 ⅛" squares
Half Square Triangle	B	3 - 1 ⅝" squares *(from each)*	3 - 1 ⅞" squares *(from each)*	3 - 2 ⅛" squares *(from each)*

Summer Moon Book by Carrie Nelson

Birds in the Air BLOCK

Piecing Instructions:

Fabric placement is intended to be scrappy.

Draw a diagonal line on the wrong side of the Fabric A squares.

With right sides facing, layer a Fabric A square with a Fabric B square.

Stitch ¼" from each side of the drawn line.

Cut apart on the marked line.

Half Square Triangle Unit should measure:

Small	1 ¼" square
Medium	1 ½" square
Large	1 ¾" square

Make thirty-six for each Block.

Assemble Block.

Birds in the Air Block should measure:

Small	5" square
Medium	6 ½" square
Large	8" square

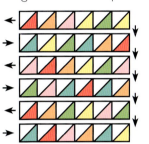 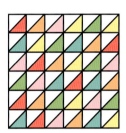

Make one Small Block.
Make one Medium Block.
Make one Large Block.

Summer Moon Book by Carrie Nelson

Buzzard's Roost BLOCK

Make 1 Small Block — 5" square unfinished
Make 1 Medium Block — 6 ½" square unfinished
Make 1 Large Block — 8" square unfinished

Make 1 Small Block — 5" square unfinished
Make 1 Medium Block — 6 ½" square unfinished
Make 1 Large Block — 8" square unfinished

Vintage Fabric Requirements:

1584-11
Fabrics A & B
⅜ yard

5080-12
Fabric C
10" x 15"

5082-11
Fabric C
10" x 15"

5084-13
Fabric C
10" x 15"

Modern Fabric Requirements:

1580-12
Fabrics A & B
⅜ yard

1680-15M
Fabric C
10" x 15"

1684-16M
Fabric C
10" x 15"

1686-17
Fabric C
10" x 15"

5085-17
Fabric C
10" x 15"

1660-20
Fabric C
10" x 15"

Cutting Instructions:

		Small Block	Medium Block	Large Block
Background	A	1 - 2" square	1 - 2 ½" square	1 - 3" square
	B	32 - 1 ¼" squares	32 - 1 ½" squares	32 - 1 ¾" squares
Flying Geese	C	4 - 1 ¼" x 2" rectangles (from each)	4 - 1 ½" x 2 ½" rectangles (from each)	4 - 1 ¾" x 3" rectangles (from each)

Summer Moon Book by Carrie Nelson

Buzzard's Roost BLOCK

Piecing Instructions:

Fabric placement is intended to be scrappy.

• •

Draw a diagonal line on the wrong side of the Fabric B squares.

With right sides facing, layer a Fabric B square on one end of a Fabric C rectangle.

Stitch on the drawn line and trim ¼" away from the seam.

Repeat on the opposite end.

Flying Geese Unit should measure:

Small	1 ¼" x 2"
Medium	1 ½" x 2 ½"
Large	1 ¾" x 3"

Make sixteen for each Block.

• •

Assemble Unit.

Double Flying Geese Unit should measure:

Small	1 ¼" x 3 ½"
Medium	1 ½" x 4 ½"
Large	1 ¾" x 5 ½"

Make four for each Block.

Assemble Unit.

Buzzard's Roost Unit should measure:

Small	3 ½" square
Medium	4 ½" square
Large	5 ½" square

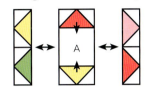

Make one for each Block.

• •

Assemble Block.

Buzzard's Roost Block should measure:

Small	5" square
Medium	6 ½" square
Large	8" square

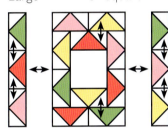 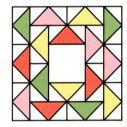

Make one Small Block.
Make one Medium Block.
Make one Large Block.

Summer Moon Book by Carrie Nelson

Capital T BLOCK

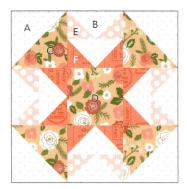

Make 1 Small Block — 5" square unfinished
Make 1 Medium Block — 6 ½" square unfinished
Make 1 Large Block — 8" square unfinished

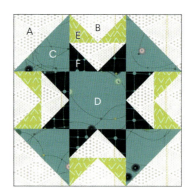

Make 1 Small Block — 5" square unfinished
Make 1 Medium Block — 6 ½" square unfinished
Make 1 Large Block — 8" square unfinished

Vintage Fabric Requirements:

1588-13
Fabrics A & B
Fat Quarter

5080-18
Fabrics C & D
Fat Eighth

5085-12
Fabric E
10" x 15"

5081-13
Fabric F
10" x 15"

Modern Fabric Requirements:

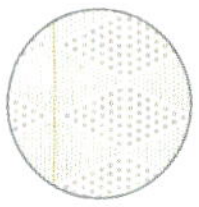

1684-11M
Fabrics A & B
Fat Quarter

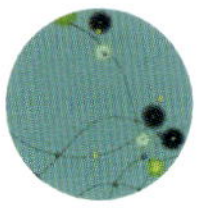

1681-16M
Fabrics C & D
Fat Eighth

1685-15
Fabric E
10" x 15"

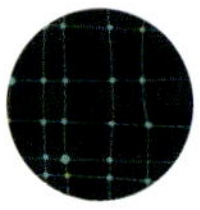

1682-22M
Fabric F
10" x 15"

Cutting Instructions:

		Small Block	Medium Block	Large Block
Background	A	2 - 2 ⅜" squares	2 - 2 ⅞" squares	2 - 3 ⅜" squares
	B	8 - 1 ¼" x 2" rectangles	8 - 1 ½" x 2 ½" rectangles	8 - 1 ¾" x 3" rectangles
Half Square Triangle and Center	C	2 - 2 ⅜" squares	2 - 2 ⅞" squares	2 - 3 ⅜" squares
	D	1 - 2" square	1 - 2 ½" square	1 - 3" square
Outer Flying Geese	E	8 - 1 ¼" squares	8 - 1 ½" squares	8 - 1 ¾" squares
Inner Flying Geese	F	8 - 1 ¼" squares	8 - 1 ½" squares	8 - 1 ¾" squares

Summer Moon Book by Carrie Nelson

Capital T BLOCK

Piecing Instructions:

Draw a diagonal line on the wrong side of the Fabric A squares.

With right sides facing, layer a Fabric A square with a Fabric C square.

Stitch ¼" from each side of the drawn line.

Cut apart on the marked line.

Half Square Triangle Unit should measure:

Small	2" square
Medium	2 ½" square
Large	3" square

Make four for each Block.

• •

Draw a diagonal line on the wrong side of the Fabric E squares.

With right sides facing, layer a Fabric E square on one end of a Fabric B rectangle.

Stitch on the drawn line and trim ¼" away from the seam.

Repeat on the opposite end.

Outer Flying Geese Unit should measure:

Small	1 ¼" x 2"
Medium	1 ½" x 2 ½"
Large	1 ¾" x 3"

Make four for each Block.

Draw a diagonal line on the wrong side of the Fabric F squares.

With right sides facing, layer a Fabric F square on one end of a Fabric B rectangle.

Stitch on the drawn line and trim ¼" away from the seam.

Repeat on the opposite end.

Inner Flying Geese Unit should measure:

Small	1 ¼" x 2"
Medium	1 ½" x 2 ½"
Large	1 ¾" x 3"

Make four for each Block.

• •

Assemble Unit.

Middle Unit should measure:

Small	2" square
Medium	2 ½" square
Large	3" square

Make four for each Block.

• •

Assemble Block.

Capital T Block should measure:

Small	5" square
Medium	6 ½" square
Large	8" square

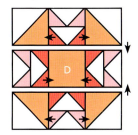 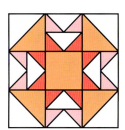

Make one Small Block.
Make one Medium Block.
Make one Large Block.

Summer Moon Book by Carrie Nelson

Checkerboard BLOCK

Make 1 Small Block — 5" square unfinished
Make 1 Medium Block — 6 ½" square unfinished
Make 1 Large Block — 8" square unfinished

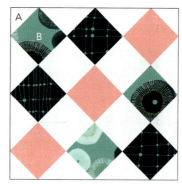

Make 1 Small Block — 5" square unfinished
Make 1 Medium Block — 6 ½" square unfinished
Make 1 Large Block — 8" square unfinished

Vintage Fabric Requirements:

29067-31 Fabric A ⅜ yard
5081-16 Fabric B 10" x 15"
5080-15 Fabric B 10" x 15"
5084-13 Fabric B 10" x 15"

Modern Fabric Requirements:

30150-101 Fabric A ⅜ yard
1680-16M Fabric B 10" x 15"
1682-22M Fabric B 10" x 15"
1660-20 Fabric B 10" x 15"

Cutting Instructions:

		Small Block	Medium Block	Large Block
Background	A	36 - 1 ¼" squares	36 - 1 ½" squares	36 - 1 ¾" squares
Diamond	B	3 - 2" squares (from each)	3 - 2 ½" squares (from each)	3 - 3" squares (from each)

18 Summer Moon Book by Carrie Nelson

Checkerboard BLOCK

Piecing Instructions:

Fabric placement is intended to be scrappy.

• •

Draw a diagonal line on the wrong side of the Fabric A squares.

With right sides facing, layer Fabric A squares on the top left and bottom right corners of a Fabric B square.

Stitch on the drawn line and trim ¼" away from the seam.

Repeat on the remaining corners.

Diamond Unit should measure:

Small   2" square
Medium   2 ½" square
Large   3" square

Make nine for each Block.

• •

Assemble Block.

Checkerboard Block should measure:

Small   5" square
Medium   6 ½" square
Large   8" square

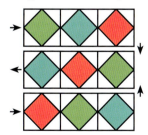 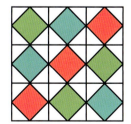

Make one Small Block.
Make one Medium Block.
Make one Large Block.

Summer Moon Book by Carrie Nelson

Churn Dash BLOCK

Make 1 Small Block — 5" square unfinished
Make 1 Medium Block — 6 ½" square unfinished
Make 1 Large Block — 8" square unfinished

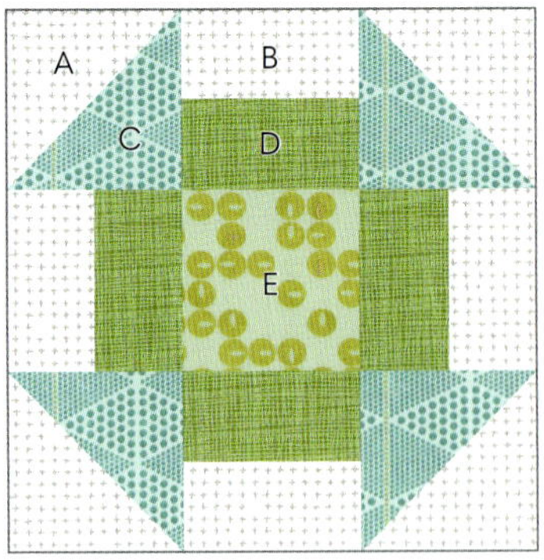

Make 1 Small Block — 5" square unfinished
Make 1 Medium Block — 6 ½" square unfinished
Make 1 Large Block — 8" square unfinished

Vintage Fabric Requirements:

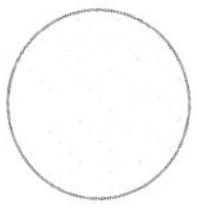

8654-59
Fabrics A & B
Fat Quarter

5080-12
Fabric C
10" x 15"

5083-18
Fabric D
10" x 15"

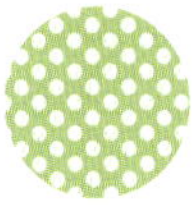

5085-16
Fabric E
10" square

Modern Fabric Requirements:

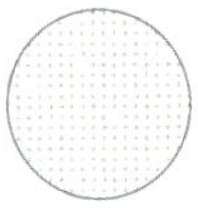

1675-13
Fabrics A & B
Fat Quarter

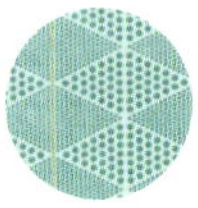

1684-16M
Fabric C
10" x 15"

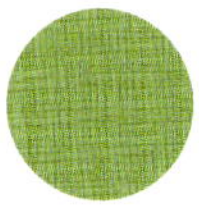

1686-14
Fabric D
10" x 15"

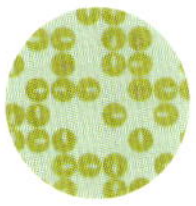

1683-16M
Fabric E
10" square

Cutting Instructions:

		Small Block	Medium Block	Large Block
Background	A	2 - 2 ⅜" squares	2 - 2 ⅞" squares	2 - 3 ⅜" squares
	B	4 - 1 ¼" x 2" rectangles	4 - 1 ½" x 2 ½" rectangles	4 - 1 ¾" x 3" rectangles
Half Square Triangle	C	2 - 2 ⅜" squares	2 - 2 ⅞" squares	2 - 3 ⅜" squares
Two Patch	D	4 - 1 ¼" x 2" rectangles	4 - 1 ½" x 2 ½" rectangles	4 - 1 ¾" x 3" rectangles
Center	E	1 - 2" square	1 - 2 ½" square	1 - 3" square

Churn Dash BLOCK

Piecing Instructions:

Draw a diagonal line on the wrong side of the Fabric A squares.

With right sides facing, layer a Fabric A square with a Fabric C square.

Stitch ¼" from each side of the drawn line.

Cut apart on the marked line.

Half Square Triangle Unit should measure:

Small	2" square
Medium	2 ½" square
Large	3" square

Make four for each Block.

• •

Assemble Unit.

Two Patch Unit should measure:

Small	2" square
Medium	2 ½" square
Large	3" square

Make four for each Block.

Assemble Block.

Churn Dash Block should measure:

Small	5" square
Medium	6 ½" square
Large	8" square

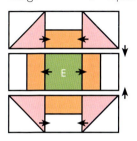 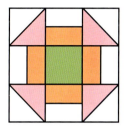

Make one Small Block.
Make one Medium Block.
Make one Large Block.

Summer Moon Book by Carrie Nelson

21

Crown of Thorns
BLOCK

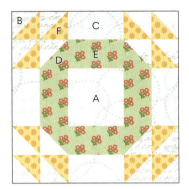

Make 1 Small Block — 5" square unfinished
Make 1 Medium Block — 6 ½" square unfinished
Make 1 Large Block — 8" square unfinished

Make 1 Small Block — 5" square unfinished
Make 1 Medium Block — 6 ½" square unfinished
Make 1 Large Block — 8" square unfinished

Vintage Fabric Requirements:

1584-11
Fabrics A to C
Fat Quarter

5082-11
Fabrics D & E
Fat Eighth

5085-17
Fabric F
10" x 15"

Modern Fabric Requirements:

1580-12
Fabrics A to C
Fat Quarter

1684-16M
Fabrics D & E
Fat Eighth

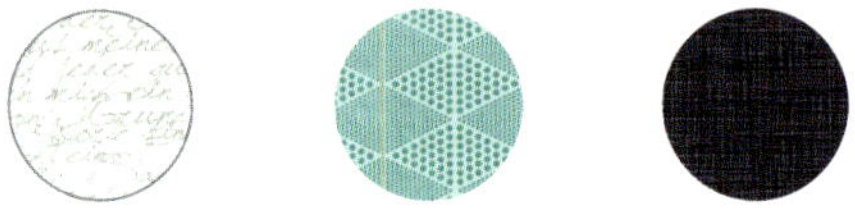

1686-17
Fabric F
10" x 15"

Cutting Instructions:

		Small Block	Medium Block	Large Block
Background	A	1 - 2" square	1 - 2 ½" square	1 - 3" square
	B	8 - 1 ⅝" squares	8 - 1 ⅞" squares	8 - 2 ⅛" squares
	C	4 - 1 ¼" x 2" rectangles	4 - 1 ½" x 2 ½" rectangles	4 - 1 ¾" x 3" rectangles
Inner Half Square Triangle and Two Patch	D	2 - 1 ⅝" squares	2 - 1 ⅞" squares	2 - 2 ⅛" squares
	E	4 - 1 ¼" x 2" rectangles	4 - 1 ½" x 2 ½" rectangles	4 - 1 ¾" x 3" rectangles
Outer Half Square Triangle	F	6 - 1 ⅝" squares	6 - 1 ⅞" squares	6 - 2 ⅛" squares

Summer Moon Book by Carrie Nelson

Crown of Thorns BLOCK

Piecing Instructions:

Draw a diagonal line on the wrong side of the Fabric B squares.

With right sides facing, layer a Fabric B square with a Fabric F square.

Stitch ¼" from each side of the drawn line.

Cut apart on the marked line.

Outer Half Square Triangle Unit should measure:

Small	1 ¼" square
Medium	1 ½" square
Large	1 ¾" square

Make twelve for each Block.

• •

With right sides facing, layer a Fabric B square with a Fabric D square.

Stitch ¼" from each side of the drawn line.

Cut apart on the marked line.

Inner Half Square Triangle Unit should measure:

Small	1 ¼" square
Medium	1 ½" square
Large	1 ¾" square

Make four for each Block.

Assemble Unit.

Corner Unit should measure:

Small	2" square
Medium	2 ½" square
Large	3" square

Make four for each Block.

• •

Assemble Unit.

Two Patch Unit should measure:

Small	2" square
Medium	2 ½" square
Large	3" square

Make four for each Block.

• •

Assemble Block.

Crown of Thorns Block should measure:

Small	5" square
Medium	6 ½" square
Large	8" square

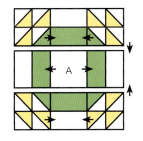 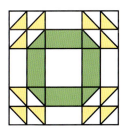

Make one Small Block.
Make one Medium Block.
Make one Large Block.

Summer Moon Book by Carrie Nelson

Darting Birds BLOCK

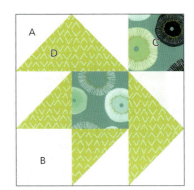

Make 1 Small Block — 5" square unfinished
Make 1 Medium Block — 6 ½" square unfinished
Make 1 Large Block — 8" square unfinished

Make 1 Small Block — 5" square unfinished
Make 1 Medium Block — 6 ½" square unfinished
Make 1 Large Block — 8" square unfinished

Vintage Fabric Requirements:

29067-31
Fabrics A & B
Fat Quarter

5085-18
Fabric C
10" x 15"

5080-18
Fabric D
Fat Eighth

Modern Fabric Requirements:

30150-101
Fabrics A & B
Fat Quarter

1680-16M
Fabric C
10" x 15"

1685-15
Fabric D
Fat Eighth

Cutting Instructions:

		Small Block	Medium Block	Large Block
Background	A	3 - 2 ⅜" squares	3 - 2 ⅞" squares	3 - 3 ⅜" squares
	B	1 - 2" square	1 - 2 ½" square	1 - 3" square
Corner and Center	C	2 - 2" squares	2 - 2 ½" squares	2 - 3" squares
Half Square Triangle	D	3 - 2 ⅜" squares	3 - 2 ⅞" squares	3 - 3 ⅜" squares

Summer Moon Book by Carrie Nelson

Darting Birds BLOCK

Piecing Instructions:

Draw a diagonal line on the wrong side of the Fabric A squares.

With right sides facing, layer a Fabric A square with a Fabric D square.

Stitch ¼" from each side of the drawn line.

Cut apart on the marked line.

Half Square Triangle Unit should measure:

Small	2" square
Medium	2 ½" square
Large	3" square

Make six for each Block.

Assemble Block.

Darting Birds Block should measure:

Small	5" square
Medium	6 ½" square
Large	8" square

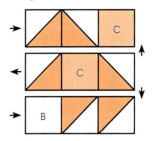 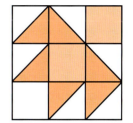

Make one Small Block.
Make one Medium Block.
Make one Large Block.

Summer Moon Book by Carrie Nelson

Fool's Puzzle BLOCK

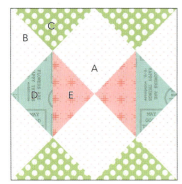

Make 1 Small Block — 5" square unfinished
Make 1 Medium Block — 6 ½" square unfinished
Make 1 Large Block — 8" square unfinished

Make 1 Small Block — 5" square unfinished
Make 1 Medium Block — 6 ½" square unfinished
Make 1 Large Block — 8" square unfinished

Vintage Fabric Requirements:

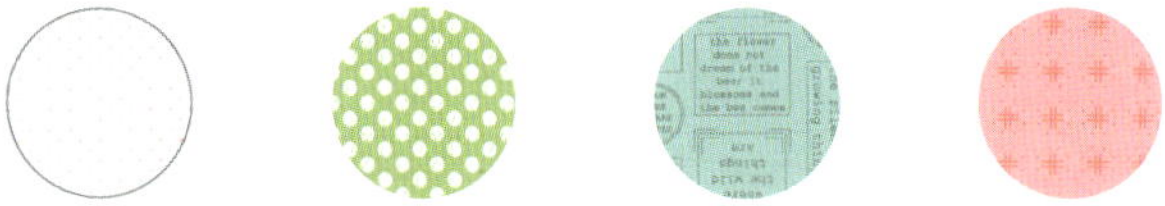

8654-59 Fabrics A & B — ⅜ yard
5085-16 Fabric C — Fat Eighth
5081-15 Fabric D — 10" x 15"
5083-12 Fabric E — Fat Eighth

Modern Fabric Requirements:

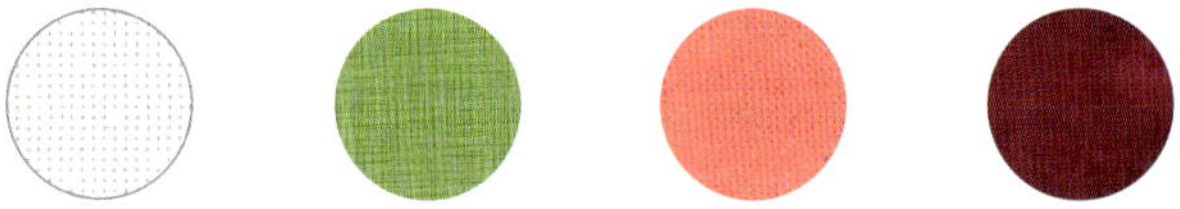

1675-13 Fabrics A & B — ⅜ yard
1686-14 Fabric C — Fat Eighth
1660-21 Fabric D — 10" x 15"
30150-63 Fabric E — Fat Eighth

Cutting Instructions:

		Small Block	Medium Block	Large Block
Background	A	1 - 3 ¾" square	1 - 4 ½" square	1 - 5 ¼" square
	B	12 - 1 ⅝" squares	12 - 2" squares	12 - 2 ⅜" squares
Outer Flying Geese	C	4 - 1 ⅝" x 2 ¾" rectangles	4 - 2" x 3 ½" rectangles	4 - 2 ⅜" x 4 ¼" rectangles
Inner Flying Geese	D	2 - 1 ⅝" x 2 ¾" rectangles	2 - 2" x 3 ½" rectangles	2 - 2 ⅜" x 4 ¼" rectangles
Hourglass	E	1 - 3 ¾" square	1 - 4 ½" square	1 - 5 ¼" square

Summer Moon Book by Carrie Nelson

Fool's Puzzle BLOCK

Piecing Instructions:

Draw a diagonal line on the wrong side of the Fabric B squares.

With right sides facing, layer a Fabric B square on one end of a Fabric C rectangle.

Stitch on the drawn line and trim ¼" away from the seam.

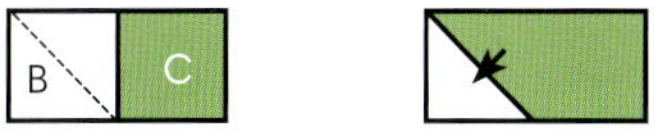

Repeat on the opposite end.

Outer Flying Geese Unit should measure:

Small	1 ⅝" x 2 ¾"
Medium	2" x 3 ½"
Large	2 ⅜" x 4 ¼"

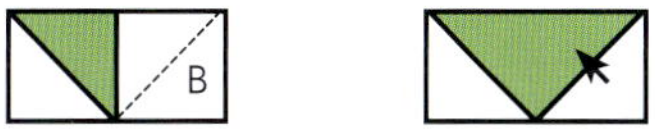

Make four for each Block.

• •

With right sides facing, layer a Fabric B square on the top end of a Fabric D rectangle.

Stitch on the drawn line and trim ¼" away from the seam.

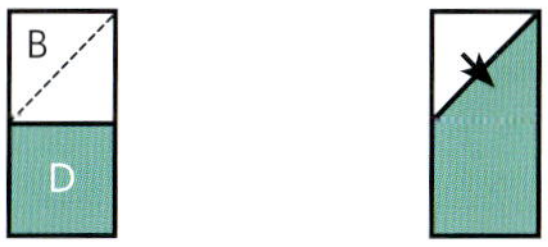

Repeat on the bottom end.

Inner Flying Geese Unit should measure:

Small	1 ⅝" x 2 ¾"
Medium	2" x 3 ½"
Large	2 ⅜" x 4 ¼"

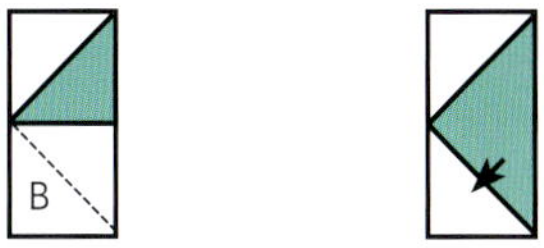

Make two for each Block.

Cut the Fabric A square and Fabric E square on the diagonal twice.

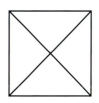 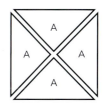 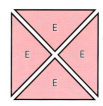

Make four Fabric A triangles for each Block.

Make four Fabric E triangles for each Block.

• •

Assemble Unit.

TRIM Hourglass Unit to measure:

Small	2 ¾" square
Medium	3 ½" square
Large	4 ¼" square

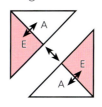

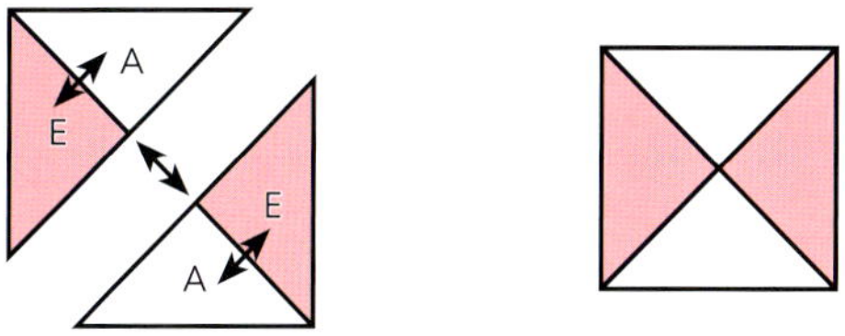

Make one for each Block.

You will not use all Fabric A and Fabric E triangles.

• •

Assemble Block.

Fool's Puzzle Block should measure:

Small	5" square
Medium	6 ½" square
Large	8" square

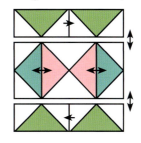 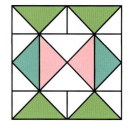

Make one Small Block.
Make one Medium Block.
Make one Large Block.

Summer Moon Book by Carrie Nelson

Four X's BLOCK

Make 1 Small Block — 5" square unfinished
Make 1 Medium Block — 6 ½" square unfinished
Make 1 Large Block — 8" square unfinished

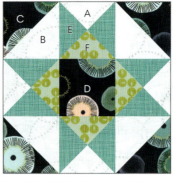

Make 1 Small Block — 5" square unfinished
Make 1 Medium Block — 6 ½" square unfinished
Make 1 Large Block — 8" square unfinished

Vintage Fabric Requirements:

1580-12
Fabrics A & B
Fat Quarter

5080-13
Fabrics C & D
Fat Eighth

5081-17
Fabric E
Fat Eighth

5083-18
Fabric F
10" x 15"

Modern Fabric Requirements:

1584-11
Fabrics A & B
Fat Quarter

1680-18M
Fabrics C & D
Fat Eighth

1686-16
Fabric E
Fat Eighth

1683-16M
Fabric F
10" x 15"

Cutting Instructions:

		Small Block	Medium Block	Large Block
Background	A	1 - 3" square	1 - 3 ½" square	1 - 4" square
	B	2 - 2 ⅜" squares	2 - 2 ⅞" squares	2 - 3 ⅜" squares
Half Square Triangle and Center	C	2 - 2 ⅜" squares	2 - 2 ⅞" squares	2 - 3 ⅜" squares
	D	1 - 2" square	1 - 2 ½" square	1 - 3" square
Outer Hourglass	E	2 - 3" squares	2 - 3 ½" squares	2 - 4" squares
Inner Hourglass	F	1 - 3" square	1 - 3 ½" square	1 - 4" square

Summer Moon Book by Carrie Nelson

Four X's BLOCK

Piecing Instructions:

Draw a diagonal line on the wrong side of the Fabric B squares.

With right sides facing, layer a Fabric B square with a Fabric C square.

Stitch ¼" from each side of the drawn line.

Cut apart on the marked line.

Half Square Triangle Unit should measure:

Small	2" square
Medium	2 ½" square
Large	3" square

Make four for each Block.

• •

Cut the Fabric A square, Fabric E squares and Fabric F square on the diagonal twice.

Make four Fabric A triangles for each Block.

Make eight Fabric E triangles for each Block.

Make four Fabric F triangles for each Block.

Assemble Unit.

TRIM Hourglass Unit to measure:

Small	2" square
Medium	2 ½" square
Large	3" square

Make four for each Block.

• •

Assemble Block.

Four X's Block should measure:

Small	5" square
Medium	6 ½" square
Large	8" square

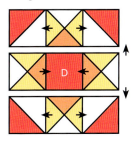 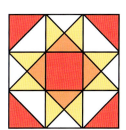

Make one Small Block.
Make one Medium Block.
Make one Large Block.

Summer Moon Book by Carrie Nelson

Friendship Star BLOCK

Make 1 Small Block — 5" square unfinished
Make 1 Medium Block — 6 ½" square unfinished
Make 1 Large Block — 8" square unfinished

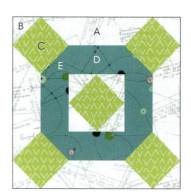

Make 1 Small Block — 5" square unfinished
Make 1 Medium Block — 6 ½" square unfinished
Make 1 Large Block — 8" square unfinished

Vintage Fabric Requirements:

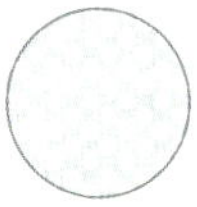

5085-11
Fabrics A & B
Fat Quarter

5080-18
Fabric C
Fat Eighth

5081-13
Fabrics D & E
Fat Eighth

Modern Fabric Requirements:

1674-18
Fabrics A & B
Fat Quarter

1685-15
Fabric C
Fat Eighth

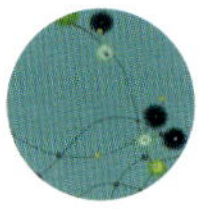

1681-16M
Fabrics D & E
Fat Eighth

Cutting Instructions:

		Small Block	Medium Block	Large Block
Background	A	4 - 1 ¼" x 2" rectangles	4 - 1 ½" x 2 ½" rectangles	4 - 1 ¾" x 3" rectangles
	B	16 - 1 ¼" squares	16 - 1 ½" squares	16 - 1 ¾" squares
Corner and Center	C	5 - 2" squares	5 - 2 ½" squares	5 - 3" squares
Corner and Two Patch	D	4 - 1 ¼" x 2" rectangles	4 - 1 ½" x 2 ½" rectangles	4 - 1 ¾" x 3" rectangles
	E	4 - 1 ¼" squares	4 - 1 ½" squares	4 - 1 ¾" squares

Summer Moon Book by Carrie Nelson

Friendship Star BLOCK

Piecing Instructions:

Draw a diagonal line on the wrong side of the Fabric B squares and Fabric E squares.

With right sides facing, layer Fabric B squares on the top right and bottom left corners of a Fabric C square.

Stitch on the drawn line and trim ¼" away from the seam.

Repeat on the top left corner with a Fabric B square and bottom right corner with a Fabric E square.

Corner Unit should measure:

  Small   2" square
  Medium   2 ½" square
  Large   3" square

Make four for each Block.

• •

With right sides facing, layer Fabric B squares on the top right and bottom left corners of a Fabric C square.

Stitch on the drawn line and trim ¼" away from the seam.

Repeat on the remaining corners.

Center Unit should measure:

  Small   2" square
  Medium   2 ½" square
  Large   3" square

Make one for each Block.

Assemble Unit.

Two Patch Unit should measure:

  Small   2" square
  Medium   2 ½" square
  Large   3" square

Make four for each Block.

• •

Assemble Block.

Friendship Star Block should measure:

  Small   5" square
  Medium   6 ½" square
  Large   8" square

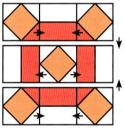 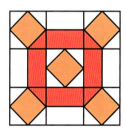

Make one Small Block.
Make one Medium Block.
Make one Large Block.

Summer Moon Book by Carrie Nelson

Hidden Star BLOCK

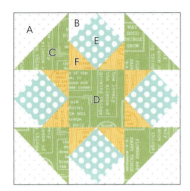

Make 1 Small Block — 5" square unfinished
Make 1 Medium Block — 6 ½" square unfinished
Make 1 Large Block — 8" square unfinished

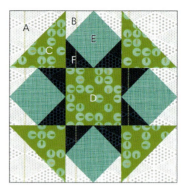

Make 1 Small Block — 5" square unfinished
Make 1 Medium Block — 6 ½" square unfinished
Make 1 Large Block — 8" square unfinished

Vintage Fabric Requirements:

1588-13 — Fabrics A & B — Fat Quarter
5081-16 — Fabrics C & D — Fat Eighth
5085-15 — Fabric E — Fat Eighth
5081-17 — Fabric F — Fat Eighth

Modern Fabric Requirements:

1684-11M — Fabrics A & B — Fat Quarter
1683-15M — Fabrics C & D — Fat Eighth
1686-16 — Fabric E — Fat Eighth
1684-18M — Fabric F — Fat Eighth

Cutting Instructions:

		Small Block	Medium Block	Large Block
Background	A	2 - 2 ⅜" squares	2 - 2 ⅞" squares	2 - 3 ⅜" squares
	B	8 - 1 ¼" squares	8 - 1 ½" squares	8 - 1 ¾" squares
Half Square Triangle and Center	C	2 - 2 ⅜" squares	2 - 2 ⅞" squares	2 - 3 ⅜" squares
	D	1 - 2" square	1 - 2 ½" square	1 - 3" square
Middle	E	4 - 2" squares	4 - 2 ½" squares	4 - 3" squares
Middle Star Points	F	8 - 1 ¼" squares	8 - 1 ½" squares	8 - 1 ¾" squares

Hidden Star BLOCK

Piecing Instructions:

Draw a diagonal line on the wrong side of the Fabric A squares.

With right sides facing, layer a Fabric A square with a Fabric C square.

Stitch ¼" from each side of the drawn line.

Cut apart on the marked line.

Half Square Triangle Unit should measure:

Small	2" square
Medium	2 ½" square
Large	3" square

Make four for each Block.

- -

Draw a diagonal line on the wrong side of the Fabric B squares and Fabric F squares.

With right sides facing, layer a Fabric B square on the top left corner and a Fabric F square on the bottom right corner of a Fabric E square.

Stitch on the drawn line and trim ¼" away from the seam.

Repeat on the top right corner with a Fabric B square and bottom left corner with a Fabric F square.

Middle Unit should measure:

Small	2" square
Medium	2 ½" square
Large	3" square

Make four for each Block.

Assemble Block.

Hidden Star Block should measure:

Small	5" square
Medium	6 ½" square
Large	8" square

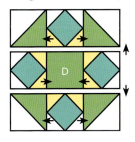 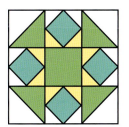

Make one Small Block.
Make one Medium Block.
Make one Large Block.

Summer Moon Book by Carrie Nelson

Log Cabin BLOCK

Make 1 Small Block — 5" square unfinished
Make 1 Medium Block — 6 ½" square unfinished
Make 1 Large Block — 8" square unfinished

Make 1 Small Block — 5" square unfinished
Make 1 Medium Block — 6 ½" square unfinished
Make 1 Large Block — 8" square unfinished

Vintage Fabric Requirements:

5081-16 Fabrics A to E Fat Eighth
5083-18 Fabrics A to E Fat Eighth
5080-12 Fabrics A to E Fat Eighth
5084-15 Fabrics A to E Fat Eighth

Modern Fabric Requirements:

1683-15M Fabrics A to E Fat Eighth
1680-16M Fabrics A to E Fat Eighth
1660-21 Fabrics A to E Fat Eighth
1686-17 Fabrics A to E Fat Eighth

Cutting Instructions:

Log Cabin		Small Block	Medium Block	Large Block
	A	1 - 1 ¾" square (from each)	1 - 2" square (from each)	1 - 2 ¼" square (from each)
	B	1 - 1" x 2 ¾" rectangle (from each)	1 - 1 ¼" x 3 ½" rectangle (from each)	1 - 1 ½" x 4 ¼" rectangle (from each)
	C	1 - 1" x 2 ¼" rectangle (from each)	1 - 1 ¼" x 2 ¾" rectangle (from each)	1 - 1 ½" x 3 ¼" rectangle (from each)
	D	1 - 1" x 2 ¼" rectangle (from each)	1 - 1 ¼" x 2 ¾" rectangle (from each)	1 - 1 ½" x 3 ¼" rectangle (from each)
	E	1 - 1" x 1 ¾" rectangle (from each)	1 - 1 ¼" x 2" rectangle (from each)	1 - 1 ½" x 2 ¼" rectangle (from each)

Summer Moon Book by Carrie Nelson

Log Cabin BLOCK

Piecing Instructions:

Fabric placement is intended to be scrappy.

• •

Assemble Unit using matching Fabric D and Fabric E rectangles.

Partial Log Cabin Unit should measure:

Small	2 ¼" square
Medium	2 ¾" square
Large	3 ¼" square

Make four for each Block.

• •

Assemble Unit using matching Fabric B and Fabric C rectangles.

Log Cabin Unit should measure:

Small	2 ¾" square
Medium	3 ½" square
Large	4 ¼" square

Make four for each Block.

Assemble Block.

Log Cabin Block should measure:

Small	5" square
Medium	6 ½" square
Large	8" square

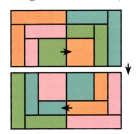 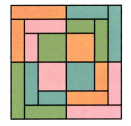

Make one Small Block.
Make one Medium Block.
Make one Large Block.

Summer Moon Book by Carrie Nelson   35

Maple Star BLOCK

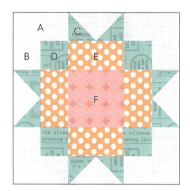

Make 1 Small Block — 5" square unfinished
Make 1 Medium Block — 6 ½" square unfinished
Make 1 Large Block — 8" square unfinished

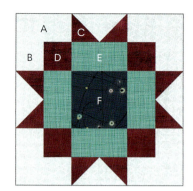

Make 1 Small Block — 5" square unfinished
Make 1 Medium Block — 6 ½" square unfinished
Make 1 Large Block — 8" square unfinished

Vintage Fabric Requirements:

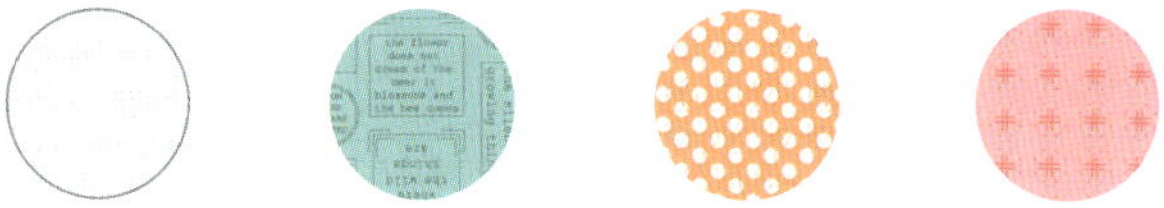

17966-20 — Fabrics A & B — Fat Quarter
5081-15 — Fabrics C & D — Fat Eighth
5085-18 — Fabric E — Fat Eighth
5083-12 — Fabric F — 10" square

Modern Fabric Requirements:

1671-22 — Fabrics A & B — Fat Quarter
30150-63 — Fabrics C & D — Fat Eighth
1686-16 — Fabric E — Fat Eighth
1681-17M — Fabric F — 10" square

Cutting Instructions:

		Small Block	Medium Block	Large Block
Background	A	8 - 1 ¼" x 2" rectangles	8 - 1 ½" x 2 ½" rectangles	8 - 1 ¾" x 3" rectangles
	B	4 - 1 ¼" squares	4 - 1 ½" squares	4 - 1 ¾" squares
Flying Geese and Corner	C	8 - 1 ¼" squares	8 - 1 ½" squares	8 - 1 ¾" squares
	D	4 - 1 ¼" squares	4 - 1 ½" squares	4 - 1 ¾" squares
Middle	E	4 - 1 ¼" x 2" rectangles	4 - 1 ½" x 2 ½" rectangles	4 - 1 ¾" x 3" rectangles
Center	F	1 - 2" square	1 - 2 ½" square	1 - 3" square

Summer Moon Book by Carrie Nelson

Maple Star BLOCK

Piecing Instructions:

Draw a diagonal line on the wrong side of the Fabric C squares.

With right sides facing, layer a Fabric C square on one end of a Fabric A rectangle.

Stitch on the drawn line and trim ¼" away from the seam.

Repeat on the opposite end.

Flying Geese Unit should measure:

Small	1 ¼" x 2"
Medium	1 ½" x 2 ½"
Large	1 ¾" x 3"

Make four for each Block.

• •

Assemble Unit.

Middle Unit should measure:

Small	2" square
Medium	2 ½" square
Large	3" square

Make four for each Block.

Assemble Unit.

Corner Unit should measure:

Small	2" square
Medium	2 ½" square
Large	3" square

Make four for each Block.

• •

Assemble Block.

Maple Star Block should measure:

Small	5" square
Medium	6 ½" square
Large	8" square

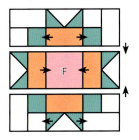   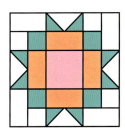

Make one Small Block.
Make one Medium Block.
Make one Large Block.

Summer Moon Book by Carrie Nelson

Memory BLOCK

Make 1 Small Block — 5" square unfinished
Make 1 Medium Block — 6 ½" square unfinished
Make 1 Large Block — 8" square unfinished

Make 1 Small Block — 5" square unfinished
Make 1 Medium Block — 6 ½" square unfinished
Make 1 Large Block — 8" square unfinished

Vintage Fabric Requirements:

1580-12 — Fabrics A to C — Fat Quarter
5084-13 — Fabrics D & E — Fat Eighth
5083-12 — Fabrics F & G — Fat Quarter
5080-15 — Fabrics H & I — Fat Eighth

Modern Fabric Requirements:

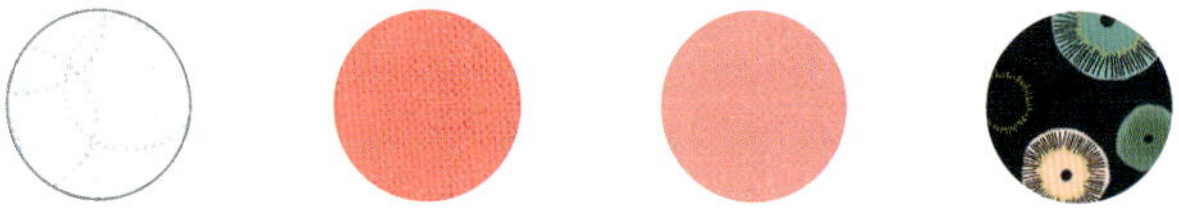

1584-11 — Fabrics A to C — Fat Quarter
1660-21 — Fabrics D & E — Fat Eighth
1660-20 — Fabrics F & G — Fat Quarter
1680-18M — Fabrics H & I — Fat Eighth

Cutting Instructions:

		Small Block	Medium Block	Large Block
Background	A	4 - 1 ⅝" squares	4 - 1 ⅞" squares	4 - 2 ⅛" squares
	B	4 - 1 ¼" x 2" rectangles	4 - 1 ½" x 2 ½" rectangles	4 - 1 ¾" x 3" rectangles
	C	4 - 1 ¼" squares	4 - 1 ½" squares	4 - 1 ¾" squares
Star Point	D	4 - 1 ⅝" squares	4 - 1 ⅞" squares	4 - 2 ⅛" squares
	E	4 - 1 ¼" squares	4 - 1 ½" squares	4 - 1 ¾" squares
Flying Geese	F	4 - 1 ¼" x 2" rectangles	4 - 1 ½" x 2 ½" rectangles	4 - 1 ¾" x 3" rectangles
	G	8 - 1 ¼" squares	8 - 1 ½" squares	8 - 1 ¾" squares
Flying Geese and Center	H	1 - 2" square	1 - 2 ½" square	1 - 3" square
	I	8 - 1 ¼" squares	8 - 1 ½" squares	8 - 1 ¾" squares

Summer Moon Book by Carrie Nelson

Memory BLOCK

Piecing Instructions:

Draw a diagonal line on the wrong side of the Fabric A squares.

With right sides facing, layer a Fabric A square with a Fabric D square.

Stitch ¼" from each side of the drawn line.

Cut apart on the marked line.

Half Square Triangle Unit should measure:

Small	1 ¼" square
Medium	1 ½" square
Large	1 ¾" square

Make eight for each Block.

• •

Assemble Unit.

Star Point Unit should measure:

Small	2" square
Medium	2 ½" square
Large	3" square

Make four for each Block.

• •

Draw a diagonal line on the wrong side of the Fabric G squares.

With right sides facing, layer a Fabric G square on one end of a Fabric B rectangle.

Stitch on the drawn line and trim ¼" away from the seam.

Repeat on the opposite end.

Outer Flying Geese Unit should measure:

Small	1 ¼" x 2"
Medium	1 ½" x 2 ½"
Large	1 ¾" x 3"

Make four for each Block.

Draw a diagonal line on the wrong side of the Fabric I squares.

With right sides facing, layer a Fabric I square on one end of a Fabric F rectangle.

Stitch on the drawn line and trim ¼" away from the seam.

Repeat on the opposite end.

Inner Flying Geese Unit should measure:

Small	1 ¼" x 2"
Medium	1 ½" x 2 ½"
Large	1 ¾" x 3"

Make four for each Block.

• •

Assemble Unit.

Middle Unit should measure:

Small	2" square
Medium	2 ½" square
Large	3" square

Make four for each Block.

• •

Assemble Block.

Memory Block should measure:

Small	5" square
Medium	6 ½" square
Large	8" square

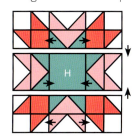 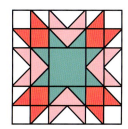

Make one Small Block.
Make one Medium Block.
Make one Large Block.

Summer Moon Book by Carrie Nelson

Nonsense BLOCK

Make 1 Small Block — 5" square unfinished
Make 1 Medium Block — 6 ½" square unfinished
Make 1 Large Block — 8" square unfinished

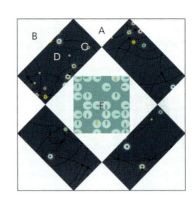

Make 1 Small Block — 5" square unfinished
Make 1 Medium Block — 6 ½" square unfinished
Make 1 Large Block — 8" square unfinished

Vintage Fabric Requirements:

29067-31
Fabrics A & B
Fat Quarter

5080-15
Fabrics C & D
Fat Quarter

5085-12
Fabric E
10" square

Modern Fabric Requirements:

30150-101
Fabrics A & B
Fat Quarter

1681-17M
Fabrics C & D
Fat Quarter

1683-17M
Fabric E
10" square

Cutting Instructions:

		Small Block	Medium Block	Large Block
Background	A	2 - 3" squares	2 - 3 ½" squares	2 - 4" squares
	B	2 - 2 ⅜" squares	2 - 2 ⅞" squares	2 - 3 ⅜" squares
Half Square Triangle and Hourglass	C	2 - 3" squares	2 - 3 ½" squares	2 - 4" squares
	D	2 - 2 ⅜" squares	2 - 2 ⅞" squares	2 - 3 ⅜" squares
Center	E	1 - 2" square	1 - 2 ½" square	1 - 3" square

Nonsense BLOCK

Piecing Instructions:

Draw a diagonal line on the wrong side of the Fabric B squares.

With right sides facing, layer a Fabric B square with a Fabric D square.

Stitch ¼" from each side of the drawn line.

Cut apart on the marked line.

Half Square Triangle Unit should measure:

Small	2" square
Medium	2 ½" square
Large	3" square

Make four for each Block.

• • • • • • • • • • • • • • • • • • • •

Draw a diagonal line on the wrong side of the Fabric A squares.

With right sides facing, layer a Fabric A square with a Fabric C square.

Stitch ¼" from each side of the drawn line.

Cut apart on the marked line.

Partial Hourglass Unit should measure:

Small	2 ⅝" square
Medium	3 ⅛" square
Large	3 ⅝" square

Make four for each Block.

Draw a diagonal line on the wrong side of two Partial Hourglass Units.

With right sides facing, layer a marked Partial Hourglass Unit with an unmarked Partial Hourglass Unit. Make sure they are turned so the seams are in the same direction.

Stitch ¼" from each side of the drawn line.

Cut apart on the marked line.

TRIM Hourglass Unit to measure:

Small	2" square
Medium	2 ½" square
Large	3" square

Make four for each Block.

• • • • • • • • • • • • • • • • • • • •

Assemble Block.

Nonsense Block should measure:

Small	5" square
Medium	6 ½" square
Large	8" square

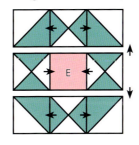 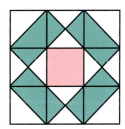

Make one Small Block.
Make one Medium Block.
Make one Large Block.

Summer Moon Book by Carrie Nelson

Patchwork Big O
BLOCK

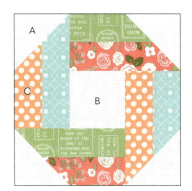

Make 1 Small Block — 5" square unfinished
Make 1 Medium Block — 6 ½" square unfinished
Make 1 Large Block — 8" square unfinished

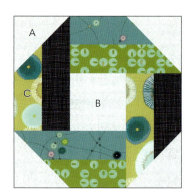

Make 1 Small Block — 5" square unfinished
Make 1 Medium Block — 6 ½" square unfinished
Make 1 Large Block — 8" square unfinished

Vintage Fabric Requirements:

17966-20 — Fabrics A & B — Fat Eighth
5080-13 — Fabric C — 10" x 15"
5081-16 — Fabric C — 10" x 15"
5084-15 — Fabric C — 10" x 15"

5085-18 — Fabric C — 10" x 15"

Modern Fabric Requirements:

1671-22 — Fabrics A & B — Fat Eighth
1680-15M — Fabric C — 10" x 15"
1681-16M — Fabric C — 10" x 15"
1683-15M — Fabric C — 10" x 15"

1686-17 — Fabric C — 10" x 15"

Cutting Instructions:

		Small Block	Medium Block	Large Block
Background	A	4 - 2" squares	4 - 2 ½" squares	4 - 3" squares
	B	1 - 2" square	1 - 2 ½" square	1 - 3" square
Big O	C	2 - 1 ¼" x 3 ½" rectangles (from each)	2 - 1 ½" x 4 ½" rectangles (from each)	2 - 1 ¾" x 5 ½" rectangles (from each)

Summer Moon Book by Carrie Nelson

Patchwork Big O BLOCK

Piecing Instructions:

Fabric placement is intended to be scrappy.

• •

Assemble Unit using different fabrics.

Two Patch Unit should measure:

Small	2" x 3 ½"
Medium	2 ½" x 4 ½"
Large	3" x 5 ½"

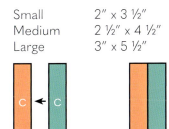

Make four for each Block.

• •

Draw a diagonal line on the wrong side of the Fabric A squares.

With right sides facing, layer a Fabric A square on the top end of a Two Patch Unit.

Stitch on the drawn line and trim ¼" away from the seam.

Big O Unit should measure:

Small	2" x 3 ½"
Medium	2 ½" x 4 ½"
Large	3" x 5 ½"

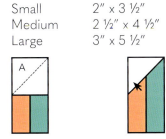

Make four for each Block.

• •

Assemble Patchwork Big O Unit One.

Start stitching ¼" away from the top edge of the Fabric B square. Backstitch.

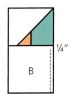 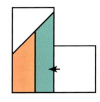

Make one for each Block.

Assemble Patchwork Big O Unit Two.

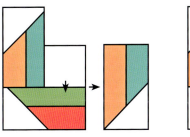 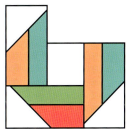

Make one for each Block.

• •

Assemble Block.

Start stitching ¼" away from the left edge of the Big O Unit. Backstitch.

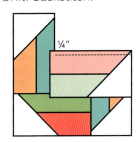

Finish assembling the Block by overlapping previous stitches.

Patchwork Big O Block should measure:

Small	5" square
Medium	6 ½" square
Large	8" square

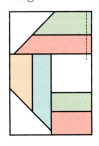 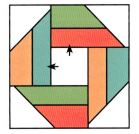

Make one Small Block.
Make one Medium Block.
Make one Large Block.

Summer Moon Book by Carrie Nelson

Pinwheel Geese BLOCK

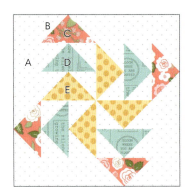

Make 1 Small Block — 5" square unfinished
Make 1 Medium Block — 6 ½" square unfinished
Make 1 Large Block — 8" square unfinished

Make 1 Small Block — 5" square unfinished
Make 1 Medium Block — 6 ½" square unfinished
Make 1 Large Block — 8" square unfinished

Vintage Fabric Requirements:

1588-13
Fabrics A & B
⅓ yard

5080-13
Fabric C
Fat Eighth

5081-15
Fabric D
Fat Eighth

5085-17
Fabric E
Fat Eighth

Modern Fabric Requirements:

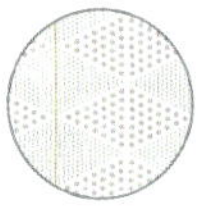

1684-11M
Fabrics A & B
⅓ yard

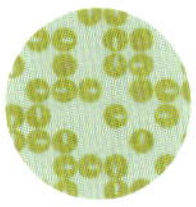

1683-16M
Fabric C
Fat Eighth

1680-16M
Fabric D
Fat Eighth

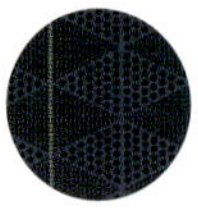

1684-18M
Fabric E
Fat Eighth

Cutting Instructions:

		Small Block	Medium Block	Large Block
Background	A	4 - 1 ¼" x 2 ¾" rectangles	4 - 1 ½" x 3 ½" rectangles	4 - 1 ¾" x 4 ¼" rectangles
	B	24 - 1 ¼" squares	24 - 1 ½" squares	24 - 1 ¾" squares
Outer Flying Geese	C	4 - 1 ¼" x 2" rectangles	4 - 1 ½" x 2 ½" rectangles	4 - 1 ¾" x 3" rectangles
Middle Flying Geese	D	4 - 1 ¼" x 2" rectangles	4 - 1 ½" x 2 ½" rectangles	4 - 1 ¾" x 3" rectangles
Inner Flying Geese	E	4 - 1 ¼" x 2" rectangles	4 - 1 ½" x 2 ½" rectangles	4 - 1 ¾" x 3" rectangles

Summer Moon Book by Carrie Nelson

Pinwheel Geese BLOCK

Piecing Instructions:

Draw a diagonal line on the wrong side of the Fabric B squares.

With right sides facing, layer a Fabric B square on one end of a Fabric C rectangle.

Stitch on the drawn line and trim ¼" away from the seam.

Repeat on the opposite end.

Outer Flying Geese Unit should measure:

Small	1 ¼" x 2"
Medium	1 ½" x 2 ½"
Large	1 ¾" x 3"

Make four for each Block.

• •

With right sides facing, layer a Fabric B square on one end of a Fabric D rectangle.

Stitch on the drawn line and trim ¼" away from the seam.

Repeat on the opposite end.

Middle Flying Geese Unit should measure:

Small	1 ¼" x 2"
Medium	1 ½" x 2 ½"
Large	1 ¾" x 3"

Make four for each Block.

With right sides facing, layer a Fabric B square on one end of a Fabric E rectangle.

Stitch on the drawn line and trim ¼" away from the seam.

Repeat on the opposite end.

Inner Flying Geese Unit should measure:

Small	1 ¼" x 2"
Medium	1 ½" x 2 ½"
Large	1 ¾" x 3"

Make four for each Block.

• •

Assemble Unit.

Pinwheel Geese Unit should measure:

Small	2 ¾" square
Medium	3 ½" square
Large	4 ¼" square

Make four for each Block.

• •

Assemble Block.

Pinwheel Geese Block should measure:

Small	5" square
Medium	6 ½" square
Large	8" square

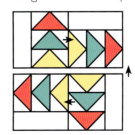 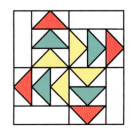

Make one Small Block.
Make one Medium Block.
Make one Large Block.

Summer Moon Book by Carrie Nelson

Rocky Mountain Puzzle BLOCK

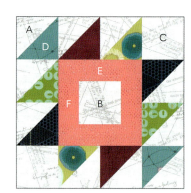

Make 1 Small Block — 5" square unfinished
Make 1 Medium Block — 6 ½" square unfinished
Make 1 Large Block — 8" square unfinished

Make 1 Small Block — 5" square unfinished
Make 1 Medium Block — 6 ½" square unfinished
Make 1 Large Block — 8" square unfinished

Vintage Fabric Requirements:

5085-11 — Fabrics A to C — Fat Quarter
5085-12 — Fabric D — 10" square
5084-15 — Fabric D — 10" square
5080-12 — Fabric D — 10" square

5085-15 — Fabric D — 10" square
5081-16 — Fabric D — 10" square
5081-15 — Fabrics E & F — 10" x 15"

Modern Fabric Requirements:

1674-18 — Fabrics A to C — Fat Quarter
1681-16M — Fabric D — 10" square
30150-63 — Fabric D — 10" square
1680-15M — Fabric D — 10" square

1684-18M — Fabric D — 10" square
1683-15M — Fabric D — 10" square
1660-21 — Fabrics E & F — 10" x 15"

Cutting Instructions:

		Small Block	Medium Block	Large Block
Background	A	5 - 2" squares	5 - 2 ⅜" squares	5 - 2 ¾" squares
	B	1 - 1 ¾" square	1 - 2" square	1 - 2 ¼" square
	C	2 - 1 ⅝" squares	2 - 2" squares	2 - 2 ⅜" squares
Half Square Triangle	D	1 - 2" square (from each)	1 - 2 ⅜" square (from each)	1 - 2 ¾" square (from each)
Center	E	2 - 1" x 2 ¾" rectangles	2 - 1 ¼" x 3 ½" rectangles	2 - 1 ½" x 4 ¼" rectangles
	F	2 - 1" x 1 ¾" rectangles	2 - 1 ¼" x 2" rectangles	2 - 1 ½" x 2 ¼" rectangles

Summer Moon Book by Carrie Nelson

Rocky Mountain Puzzle BLOCK

Piecing Instructions:

Fabric placement is intended to be scrappy.

• •

Draw a diagonal line on the wrong side of the Fabric A squares.

With right sides facing, layer a Fabric A square with a Fabric D square.

Stitch ¼" from each side of the drawn line.

Cut apart on the marked line.

Half Square Triangle Unit should measure:

Small	1 ⅝" square
Medium	2" square
Large	2 ⅜" square

Make ten for each Block.

• •

Assemble Unit.

Center Unit should measure:

Small	2 ¾" square
Medium	3 ½" square
Large	4 ¼" square

Make one for each Block.

• •

Assemble Unit.

Rocky Mountain Puzzle Unit should measure:

Small	2 ¾" x 5"
Medium	3 ½" x 6 ½"
Large	4 ¼" x 8"

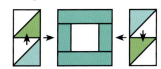 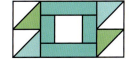

Make one for each Block.

Assemble Block.

Rocky Mountain Puzzle Block should measure:

Small	5" square
Medium	6 ½" square
Large	8" square

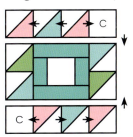 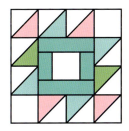

Make one Small Block.
Make one Medium Block.
Make one Large Block.

Summer Moon Book by Carrie Nelson   47

Southern Star BLOCK

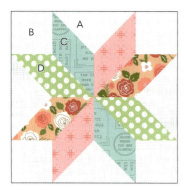

Make 1 Small Block — 5" square unfinished
Make 1 Medium Block — 6 ½" square unfinished
Make 1 Large Block — 8" square unfinished

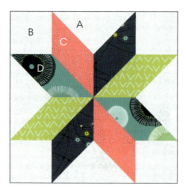

Make 1 Small Block — 5" square unfinished
Make 1 Medium Block — 6 ½" square unfinished
Make 1 Large Block — 8" square unfinished

Vintage Fabric Requirements:

17966-20
Fabrics A & B
Fat Quarter

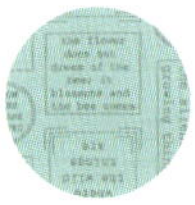

5081-15
Fabric C
10" x 15"

5080-18
Fabric C
10" x 15"

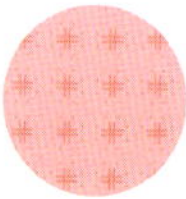

5083-12
Fabric D
10" x 15"

5085-16
Fabric D
10" x 15"

Modern Fabric Requirements:

1671-22
Fabrics A & B
Fat Quarter

1660-21
Fabric C
10" x 15"

1685-15
Fabric C
10" x 15"

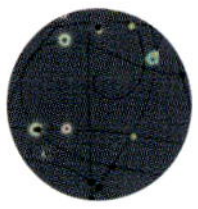

1681-17M
Fabric D
10" x 15"

1680-16M
Fabric D
10" x 15"

Cutting Instructions:

		Small Block	Medium Block	Large Block
Background	A	4 - 2" squares	4 - 2 ⅜" squares	4 - 2 ¾" squares
	B	4 - 1 ⅝" squares	4 - 2" squares	4 - 2 ⅜" squares
Star Point One	C	2 - 2" squares (from each)	2 - 2 ⅜" squares (from each)	2 - 2 ¾" squares (from each)
Star Point Two	D	2 - 2" squares (from each)	2 - 2 ⅜" squares (from each)	2 - 2 ¾" squares (from each)

Summer Moon Book by Carrie Nelson

Southern Star BLOCK

Piecing Instructions:

Draw a diagonal line on the wrong side of the Fabric A squares.

With right sides facing, layer a Fabric A square with a Fabric C square.

Stitch ¼" from each side of the drawn line.

Cut apart on the marked line.

Outer Star Point One Unit should measure:

Small	1 ⅝" square
Medium	2" square
Large	2 ⅜" square

Make two for each Block.   Make two for each Block.

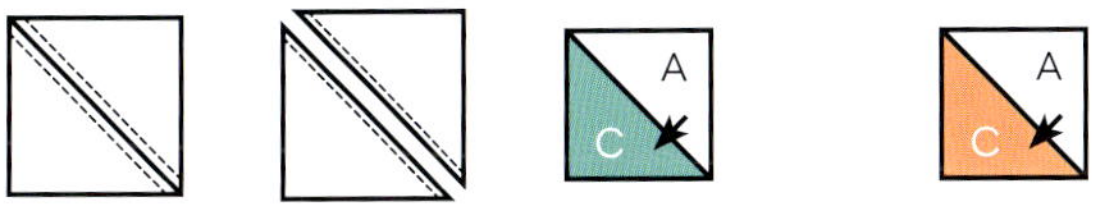

With right sides facing, layer a Fabric A square with a Fabric D square.

Stitch ¼" from each side of the drawn line.

Cut apart on the marked line.

Outer Star Point Two Unit should measure:

Small	1 ⅝" square
Medium	2" square
Large	2 ⅜" square

Make two for each Block.   Make two for each Block.

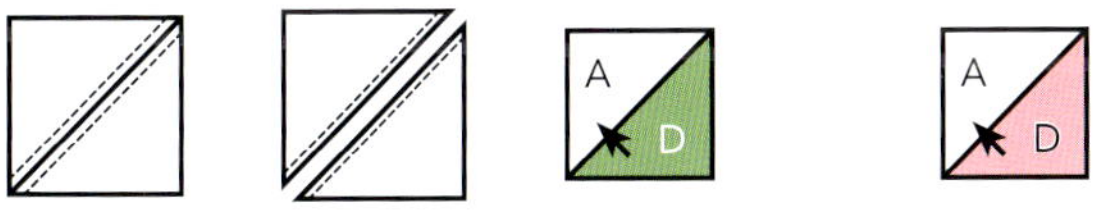

Draw a diagonal line on the wrong side of the remaining Fabric C squares.

With right sides facing, layer a Fabric C square with a coordinating Fabric D square.

Stitch ¼" from each side of the drawn line.

Cut apart on the marked line.

Inner Star Point Unit should measure:

Small	1 ⅝" square
Medium	2" square
Large	2 ⅜" square

Make two for each Block.   Make two for each Block.

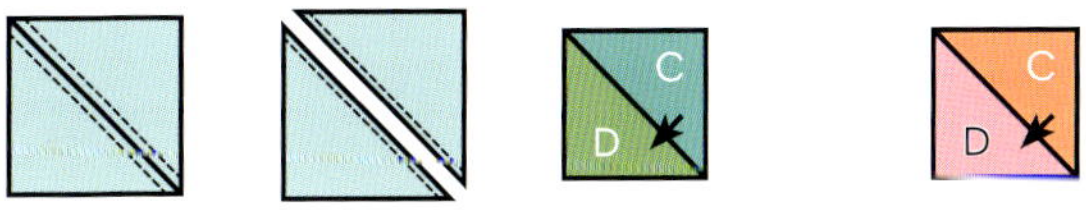

Assemble Unit using coordinating fabric.

Southern Star Unit should measure:

Small	2 ¾" square
Medium	3 ½" square
Large	4 ¼" square

Make two for each Block.   Make two for each Block.

Assemble Block.

Southern Star Block should measure:

Small	5" square
Medium	6 ½" square
Large	8" square

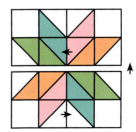 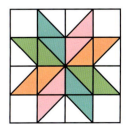

Make one Small Block.
Make one Medium Block.
Make one Large Block.

Summer Moon Book by Carrie Nelson   49

Split Nine Patch BLOCK

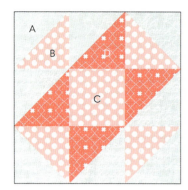

Make 1 Small Block — 5" square unfinished
Make 1 Medium Block — 6 ½" square unfinished
Make 1 Large Block — 8" square unfinished

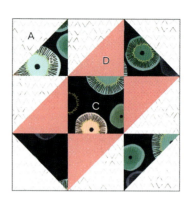

Make 1 Small Block — 5" square unfinished
Make 1 Medium Block — 6 ½" square unfinished
Make 1 Large Block — 8" square unfinished

Vintage Fabric Requirements:

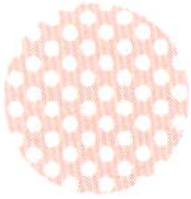

1580-11 Fabric A Fat Eighth
5085-12 Fabrics B & C Fat Eighth
5084-13 Fabric D 10" x 15"

Modern Fabric Requirements:

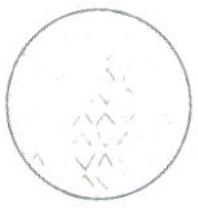

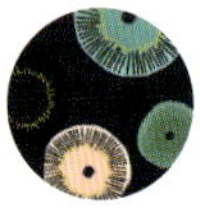

1685-11 Fabric A Fat Eighth
1680-18M Fabrics B & C Fat Eighth
1660-20 Fabric D 10" x 15"

Cutting Instructions:

		Small Block	Medium Block	Large Block
Background	A	4 - 2 ⅜" squares	4 - 2 ⅞" squares	4 - 3 ⅜" squares
Corner Half Square Triangle and Center	B	2 - 2 ⅜" squares	2 - 2 ⅞" squares	2 - 3 ⅜" squares
	C	1 - 2" square	1 - 2 ½" square	1 - 3" square
Middle Half Square Triangle	D	2 - 2 ⅜" squares	2 - 2 ⅞" squares	2 - 3 ⅜" squares

Summer Moon Book by Carrie Nelson

Split Nine Patch BLOCK

Piecing Instructions:

Draw a diagonal line on the wrong side of the Fabric A squares.

With right sides facing, layer a Fabric A square with a Fabric B square.

Stitch ¼" from each side of the drawn line.

Cut apart on the marked line.

Corner Half Square Triangle Unit should measure:

Small	2" square
Medium	2 ½" square
Large	3" square

Make four for each Block.

With right sides facing, layer a Fabric A square with a Fabric D square.

Stitch ¼" from each side of the drawn line.

Cut apart on the marked line.

Middle Half Square Triangle Unit should measure:

Small	2" square
Medium	2 ½" square
Large	3" square

Make four for each Block.

Assemble Block.

Split Nine Patch Block should measure:

Small	5" square
Medium	6 ½" square
Large	8" square

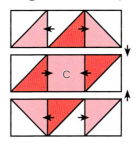 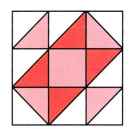

Make one Small Block.
Make one Medium Block.
Make one Large Block.

Summer Moon Book by Carrie Nelson

Twin Star BLOCK

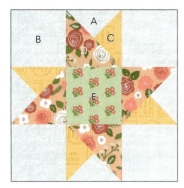

Make 1 Small Block — 5" square unfinished
Make 1 Medium Block — 6 ½" square unfinished
Make 1 Large Block — 8" square unfinished

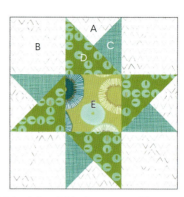

Make 1 Small Block — 5" square unfinished
Make 1 Medium Block — 6 ½" square unfinished
Make 1 Large Block — 8" square unfinished

Vintage Fabric Requirements:

1580-11 — Fabrics A & B — Fat Quarter
5081-17 — Fabric C — 10" x 15"
5080-18 — Fabric D — 10" x 15"
5082-11 — Fabric E — 10" square

Modern Fabric Requirements:

1685-11 — Fabrics A & B — Fat Quarter
1686-16 — Fabric C — 10" x 15"
1683-15M — Fabric D — 10" x 15"
1680-15M — Fabric E — 10" square

Cutting Instructions:

		Small Block	Medium Block	Large Block
Background	A	1 - 3" square	1 - 3 ½" square	1 - 4" square
	B	4 - 2" squares	4 - 2 ½" squares	4 - 3" squares
Outer Star Point	C	1 - 3" square	1 - 3 ½" square	1 - 4" square
Inner Star Point	D	2 - 2 ½" squares	2 - 3" squares	2 - 3 ½" squares
Center	E	1 - 2" square	1 - 2 ½" square	1 - 3" square

Summer Moon Book by Carrie Nelson

Twin Star BLOCK

Piecing Instructions:

Cut the Fabric A square and Fabric C square on the diagonal twice.

Make four Fabric A triangles for each Block.
Make four Fabric C triangles for each Block.

• •

Cut the Fabric D squares on the diagonal once.

Make four for each Block.

• •

Assemble Unit.

TRIM Star Point Unit to measure:

  Small   2" square
  Medium   2 ½" square
  Large   3" square

Make four for each Block.

Assemble Block.
Twin Star Block should measure:

  Small   5" square
  Medium   6 ½" square
  Large   8" square

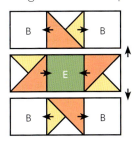 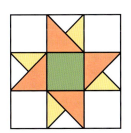

Make one Small Block.
Make one Medium Block.
Make one Large Block.

Summer Moon Book by Carrie Nelson 53

Weathervane BLOCK

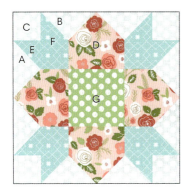

Make 1 Small Block — 5" square unfinished
Make 1 Medium Block — 6 ½" square unfinished
Make 1 Large Block — 8" square unfinished

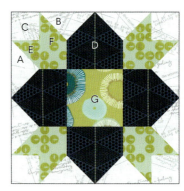

Make 1 Small Block — 5" square unfinished
Make 1 Medium Block — 6 ½" square unfinished
Make 1 Large Block — 8" square unfinished

Vintage Fabric Requirements:

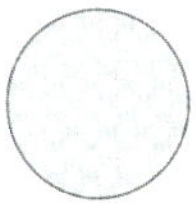

5085-11 Fabrics A to C Fat Quarter
5080-12 Fabric D Fat Eighth 
5084-15 Fabrics E & F Fat Eighth 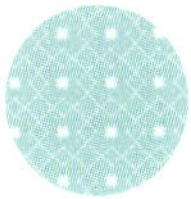
5085-16 Fabric G 10" square 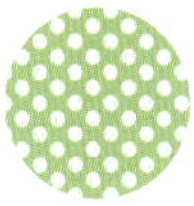

Modern Fabric Requirements:

1674-18 Fabrics A to C Fat Quarter
1684-18M Fabric D Fat Eighth 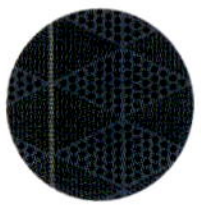
1683-16M Fabrics E & F Fat Eighth 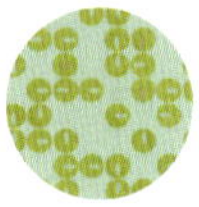
1680-15M Fabric G 10" square 

Cutting Instructions:

		Small Block	Medium Block	Large Block
Background	A	2 - 1 ⅝" squares	2 - 1 ⅞" squares	2 - 2 ⅛" squares
	B	12 - 1 ¼" squares	12 - 1 ½" squares	12 - 1 ¾" squares
	C	4 - 1 ¼" squares	4 - 1 ½" squares	4 - 1 ¾" squares
Middle	D	4 - 2" squares	4 - 2 ½" squares	4 - 3" squares
Star Point	E	2 - 1 ⅝" squares	2 - 1 ⅞" squares	2 - 2 ⅛" squares
	F	4 - 1 ¼" x 2" rectangles	4 - 1 ½" x 2 ½" rectangles	4 - 1 ¾" x 3" rectangles
Center	G	1 - 2" square	1 - 2 ½" square	1 - 3" square

Summer Moon Book by Carrie Nelson

Weathervane BLOCK

Piecing Instructions:

Draw a diagonal line on the wrong side of the Fabric A squares.

With right sides facing, layer a Fabric A square with a Fabric E square.

Stitch ¼" from each side of the drawn line.

Cut apart on the marked line.

Half Square Triangle Unit should measure:

Small	1 ¼" square
Medium	1 ½" square
Large	1 ¾" square

Make four for each Block.

• •

Draw a diagonal line on the wrong side of the Fabric B squares.

With right sides facing, layer a Fabric B square on the top end of a Fabric F rectangle.

Stitch on the drawn line and trim ¼" away from the seam.

Partial Star Point Unit should measure:

Small	1 ¼" x 2"
Medium	1 ½" x 2 ½"
Large	1 ¾" x 3"

Make four for each Block.

• •

Assemble Unit.

Star Point Unit should measure:

Small	2" square
Medium	2 ½" square
Large	3" square

Make four for each Block.

With right sides facing, layer a Fabric B square on the top left corner of a Fabric D square.

Stitch on the drawn line and trim ¼" away from the seam.

Repeat on the top right corner.

Middle Unit should measure:

Small	2" square
Medium	2 ½" square
Large	3" square

Make four for each Block.

• •

Assemble Block.

Weathervane Block should measure:

Small	5" square
Medium	6 ½" square
Large	8" square

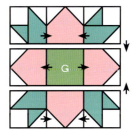 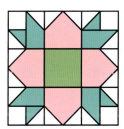

Make one Small Block.
Make one Medium Block.
Make one Large Block.

Summer Moon Book by Carrie Nelson

Framed Blocks
CHEAT SHEET

There are different framing options for the blocks which serve two purposes. They make the blocks the same finished size and allow them to float. The Small Blocks have four setting options, and the Medium and Large Blocks have one setting option each.

SMALL CORNER TRIANGLE FRAMED BLOCK

SMALL HALF SQUARE TRIANGLE FRAMED BLOCK

SMALL PATCHWORK FRAMED BLOCK

SMALL THREE GEESE FRAMED BLOCK

MEDIUM BACKGROUND FRAMED BLOCK

LARGE BACKGROUND FRAMED BLOCK

Summer Moon Book by Carrie Nelson

Framed Blocks
CHEAT SHEET

To make the Summer Moon Quilt exactly as pictured, follow the chart below. The background SKUs used in each block are listed for reference.

VINTAGE BACKGROUND SKU	MODERN BACKGROUND SKU	BLOCK NAME	FRAMED BLOCK NAME
8654-59	1675-13	Album Block Churn Dash Block Fool's Puzzle Block	Small Corner Triangle Framed Block Medium Background Framed Block Large Background Framed Block
1588-13	1684-11M	Capital T Block Hidden Star Block Pinwheel Geese Block	Small Corner Triangle Framed Block Medium Background Framed Block Large Background Framed Block
1584-11	1580-12	Bear's Track Block Buzzard's Roost Block Crown of Thorns Block	Small Half Square Triangle Framed Block Medium Background Framed Block Large Background Framed Block
1580-11	1685-11	Birds in the Air Block Split Nine Patch Block Twin Star Block	Small Half Square Triangle Framed Block Medium Background Framed Block Large Background Framed Block
17966-20	1671-22	Maple Star Block Patchwork Big O Block Southern Star Block	Small Patchwork Framed Block Medium Background Framed Block Large Background Framed Block
29067-31	30150-101	Checkerboard Block Darting Birds Block Nonsense Block	Small Patchwork Framed Block Medium Background Framed Block Large Background Framed Block
1580-12	1584-11	Four X's Block Log Cabin Block Memory Block	Small Three Geese Framed Block Medium Background Framed Block Large Background Framed Block
5085-11	1674-18	Friendship Star Block Rocky Mountain Puzzle Block Weathervane Block	Small Three Geese Framed Block Medium Background Framed Block Large Background Framed Block

Summer Moon Book by Carrie Nelson

Small Corner Triangle
FRAMED BLOCK

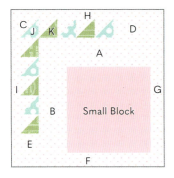

Make 3
8 ¾" square unfinished

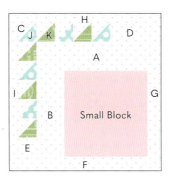

Make 3
8 ¾" square unfinished

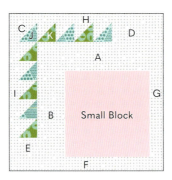

Make 3
8 ¾" square unfinished

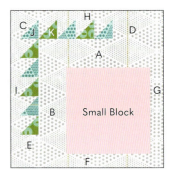

Make 3
8 ¾" square unfinished

Vintage Fabric Requirements:

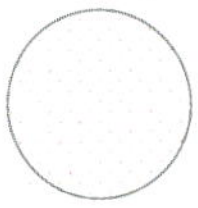

8654-59
Fabrics A to I
⅜ yard

1588-13
Fabrics A to I
⅜ yard

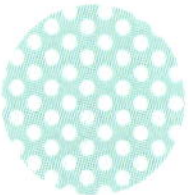

5085-15
Fabric J
10" x 15"

5081-16
Fabric K
10" x 15"

Modern Fabric Requirements:

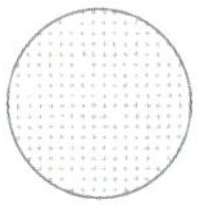

1675-13
Fabrics A to I
⅜ yard

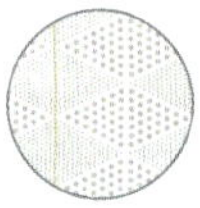

1684-11M
Fabrics A to I
⅜ yard

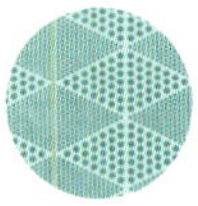

1684-16M
Fabric J
10" x 15"

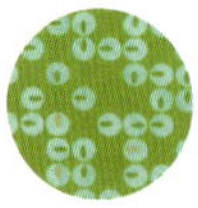

1683-15M
Fabric K
10" x 15"

Cutting Instructions:

	Complete Quilt
Background	A 3 - 2" x 6 ½" rectangles *(from each)*
	B 3 - 2" x 5" rectangles *(from each)*
	C 16 - 1 ⅞" squares *(from each)*
	D 3 - 1 ½" x 2 ½" rectangles *(from each)*
	E 3 - 1 ½" squares *(from each)*
	F 3 - 1 ¼" x 8 ¾" rectangles *(from each)*
	G 3 - 1 ¼" x 7 ½" rectangles *(from each)*
	H 3 - 1" x 8 ¾" rectangles *(from each)*
	I 3 - 1" x 7 ½" rectangles *(from each)*
Half Square Triangle One	J 16 - 1 ⅞" squares
Half Square Triangle Two	K 16 - 1 ⅞" squares

Small Corner Triangle FRAMED BLOCK

Piecing Instructions:

Draw a diagonal line on the wrong side of the Fabric C squares.

With right sides facing, layer a Fabric C square with a Fabric J square.

Stitch ¼" from each side of the drawn line.

Cut apart on the marked line.

Half Square Triangle One Unit should measure 1 ½" x 1 ½".

Make sixteen from each background.   Make sixteen from each background.

Make thirty-two total.

• •

With right sides facing, layer a Fabric C square with a Fabric K square.

Stitch ¼" from each side of the drawn line.

Cut apart on the marked line.

Half Square Triangle Two Unit should measure 1 ½" x 1 ½".

Make sixteen from each background.   Make sixteen from each background.

Make thirty-two total.

• •

Assemble Unit using matching background fabric.

Partial Center Unit should measure 6 ½" x 6 ½".

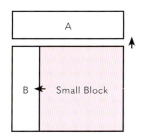 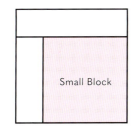

Make six total.

Assemble Unit using matching background fabric.

Center Unit should measure 7 ½" x 7 ½".

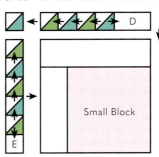 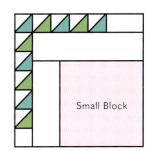

Make six total.

You will not use all Half Square Triangle Units.

• •

Assemble Block using matching background fabric.

Small Corner Triangle Framed Block should measure 8 ¾" x 8 ¾".

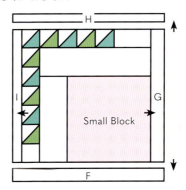

Make six Blocks.

 Summer Moon Book by Carrie Nelson

Small Half Square Triangle
FRAMED BLOCK

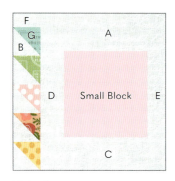
Make 3
8 ¾" square unfinished

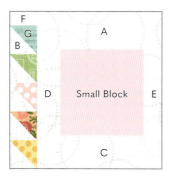
Make 3
8 ¾" square unfinished

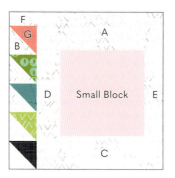
Make 3
8 ¾" square unfinished

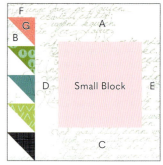
Make 3
8 ¾" square unfinished

Vintage Fabric Requirements:

1580-11
Fabrics A to F
⅜ yard

1584-11
Fabrics A to F
⅜ yard

5080-18
Fabric G
10" square

5081-15
Fabric G
10" square

5081-16
Fabric G
10" square

5085-12
Fabric G
10" square

5085-17
Fabric G
10" square

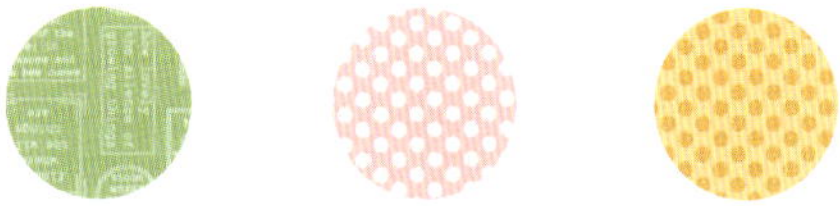

Modern Fabric Requirements:

1685-11
Fabrics A to F
⅜ yard

1580-12
Fabrics A to F
⅜ yard

1681-16M
Fabric G
10" square

1683-15M
Fabric G
10" square

1685-15
Fabric G
10" square

1686-17
Fabric G
10" square

1660-21
Fabric G
10" square

Cutting Instructions:

	Complete Quilt	
Background	A	3 - 2 ½" x 7 ¼" rectangles *(from each)*
	B	10 - 2 ⅜" squares *(from each)*
	C	3 - 2 ¼" x 7 ¼" rectangles *(from each)*
	D	3 - 1 ¾" x 5" rectangles *(from each)*
	E	3 - 1 ½" x 5" rectangles *(from each)*
	F	3 - 1 ¼" x 2" rectangles *(from each)*
Half Square Triangle	G	4 - 2 ⅜" squares *(from each)*

Summer Moon Book by Carrie Nelson

Small Half Square Triangle FRAMED BLOCK

Piecing Instructions:

Fabric placement is intended to be scrappy.

• •

Draw a diagonal line on the wrong side of the Fabric B squares.

With right sides facing, layer a Fabric B square with a Fabric G square.

Stitch ¼" from each side of the drawn line.

Cut apart on the marked line.

Half Square Triangle Unit should measure 2" x 2".

Make twenty from each background.

Make forty total.

• •

Assemble Unit using matching background fabric.

Left Framed Unit should measure 2" x 8 ¾".

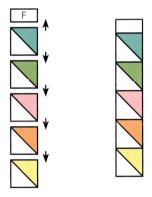

Make three from each background.

Make six total.

You will not use all Half Square Triangle Units.

Assemble Unit using matching background fabric.

Center Unit should measure 7 ¼" x 8 ¾".

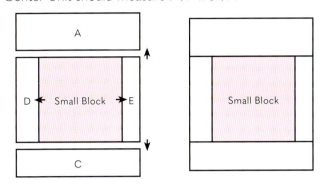

Make six total.

• •

Assemble Block using matching background fabric.

Small Half Square Triangle Framed Block should measure 8 ¾" x 8 ¾".

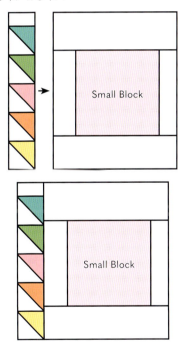

Make six Blocks.

Summer Moon Book by Carrie Nelson

Small Patchwork FRAMED BLOCK

Make 3
8 ¾" square unfinished

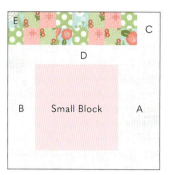

Make 3
8 ¾" square unfinished

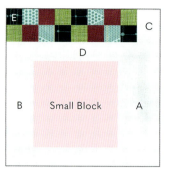

Make 3
8 ¾" square unfinished

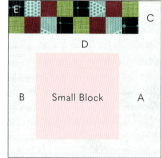

Make 3
8 ¾" square unfinished

Vintage Fabric Requirements:

29067-31
Fabrics A to D
Fat Quarter

17966-20
Fabrics A to D
Fat Quarter

5080-15
Fabric E
10" x 15"

5082-11
Fabric E
10" x 15"

5083-12
Fabric E
10" x 15"

5085-16
Fabric E
10" x 15"

Modern Fabric Requirements:

30150-101
Fabrics A to D
Fat Quarter

1671-22
Fabrics A to D
Fat Quarter

1682-22M
Fabric E
10" x 15"

1684-16M
Fabric E
10" x 15"

1686-14
Fabric E
10" x 15"

30150-63
Fabric E
10" x 15"

Cutting Instructions:

	Complete Quilt	
Background	A	3 - 2 ¾" x 5" rectangles *(from each)*
	B	3 - 2" x 5" rectangles *(from each)*
	C	3 - 1 ¾" x 2 ¼" rectangles *(from each)*
	D	6 - 1 ½" x 8 ¾" rectangles *(from each)*
Patchwork	E	24 - 1 ⅜" squares *(from each)*

Summer Moon Book by Carrie Nelson

Small Patchwork FRAMED BLOCK

Piecing Instructions:

Fabric placement is intended to be scrappy.

Assemble Unit.
Patchwork Unit should measure 2 ¼" x 7 ½".

Make six total.

Assemble Block using matching background fabric.
Small Patchwork Framed Block should measure 8 ¾" x 8 ¾".

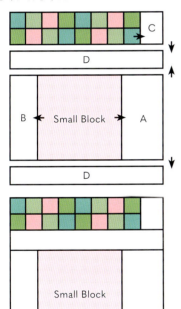

Make six Blocks.

Summer Moon Book by Carrie Nelson

Small Three Geese
FRAMED BLOCK

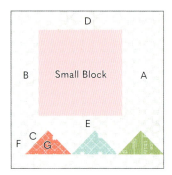 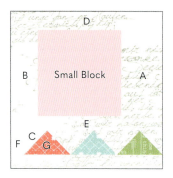 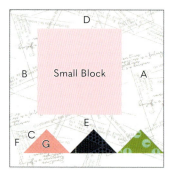 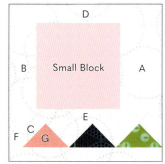

Make 3
8 ¾" square unfinished

Make 3
8 ¾" square unfinished

Make 3
8 ¾" square unfinished

Make 3
8 ¾" square unfinished

Vintage Fabric Requirements:

5085-11
Fabrics A to F
Fat Quarter

1580-12
Fabrics A to F
Fat Quarter

5081-16
Fabric G
10" square

5084-13
Fabric G
10" square

Modern Fabric Requirements:

1674-18
Fabrics A to F
Fat Quarter

1584-11
Fabrics A to F
Fat Quarter

1684-18M
Fabric G
10" square

1683-15M
Fabric G
10" square

5084-15
Fabric G
10" square

1660-20
Fabric G
10" square

Cutting Instructions:

		Complete Quilt
Background	A	3 - 2 ¾" x 5" rectangles *(from each)*
	B	3 - 2" x 5" rectangles *(from each)*
	C	18 - 1 ¾" squares *(from each)*
	D	3 - 1 ½" x 8 ¾" rectangles *(from each)*
	E	6 - 1 ¼" x 8 ¾" rectangles *(from each)*
	F	3 - 1 ¼" x 1 ¾" rectangles *(from each)*
Flying Geese	G	6 - 1 ¾" x 3" rectangles *(from each)*

Small Three Geese
FRAMED BLOCK

Piecing Instructions:
Fabric placement is intended to be scrappy.

• •

Draw a diagonal line on the wrong side of the Fabric C squares.

With right sides facing, layer a Fabric C square on one end of a Fabric G rectangle.

Stitch on the drawn line and trim ¼" away from the seam.

Repeat on the opposite end with a matching Fabric C square.

Flying Geese Unit should measure 1 ¾" x 3".

Make nine from each background.

Make eighteen total.

Assemble Block using matching background fabric.

Small Three Geese Framed Block should measure 8 ¾" x 8 ¾".

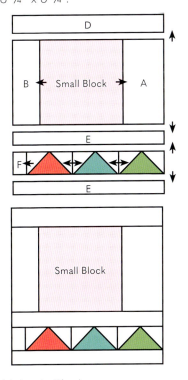

Make six Blocks.

Summer Moon Book by Carrie Nelson

Medium Background
FRAMED BLOCK

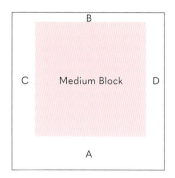

Make 24 total
8 ¾" square unfinished

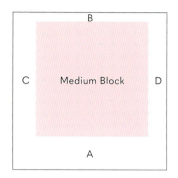

Make 24 total
8 ¾" square unfinished

Vintage Fabric Requirements:

5085-11 | 1580-11 | 1580-12 | 1584-11
Fabrics A to D | Fabrics A to D | Fabrics A to D | Fabrics A to D
Fat Quarter | Fat Quarter | Fat Quarter | Fat Quarter

1588-13 | 8654-59 | 17966-20 | 29067-31
Fabrics A to D | Fabrics A to D | Fabrics A to D | Fabrics A to D
Fat Quarter | Fat Quarter | Fat Quarter | Fat Quarter

Modern Fabric Requirements:

1684-11M | 1685-11 | 1580-12 | 1584-11
Fabrics A to D | Fabrics A to D | Fabrics A to D | Fabrics A to D
Fat Quarter | Fat Quarter | Fat Quarter | Fat Quarter

1671-22 | 1674-18 | 1675-13 | 30150-101
Fabrics A to D | Fabrics A to D | Fabrics A to D | Fabrics A to D
Fat Quarter | Fat Quarter | Fat Quarter | Fat Quarter

Cutting Instructions:

	Complete Quilt
Background	A 3 - 2 ¼" x 8 ¾" rectangles (from each)
	B 3 - 1" x 8 ¾" rectangles (from each)
	C 3 - 1 ¾" x 6 ½" rectangles (from each)
	D 3 - 1 ½" x 6 ½" rectangles (from each)

Summer Moon Book by Carrie Nelson

Medium Background
FRAMED BLOCK

Piecing Instructions:

Assemble Block using matching background fabric.

Medium Background Framed Block should measure 8 ¾" x 8 ¾".

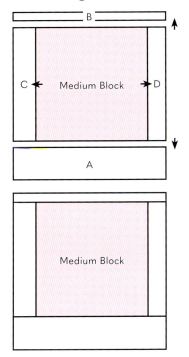

Make twenty-four Blocks.

Summer Moon Book by Carrie Nelson

Large Background
FRAMED BLOCK

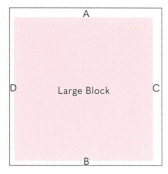

Make 24 total
8 ¾" square unfinished

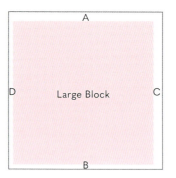

Make 24 total
8 ¾" square unfinished

Vintage Fabric Requirements:

5085-11 | 1580-11 | 1580-12 | 1584-11
Fabrics A to D | Fabrics A to D | Fabrics A to D | Fabrics A to D
Fat Quarter | Fat Quarter | Fat Quarter | Fat Quarter

1588-13 | 8654-59 | 17966-20 | 29067-31
Fabrics A to D | Fabrics A to D | Fabrics A to D | Fabrics A to D
Fat Quarter | Fat Quarter | Fat Quarter | Fat Quarter

Modern Fabric Requirements:

1684-11M | 1685-11 | 1580-12 | 1584-11
Fabrics A to D | Fabrics A to D | Fabrics A to D | Fabrics A to D
Fat Quarter | Fat Quarter | Fat Quarter | Fat Quarter

1671-22 | 1674-18 | 1675-13 | 30150-101
Fabrics A to D | Fabrics A to D | Fabrics A to D | Fabrics A to D
Fat Quarter | Fat Quarter | Fat Quarter | Fat Quarter

Cutting Instructions:

	Complete Quilt
Background	A 3 - 1" x 8 ¾" rectangles *(from each)*
	B 3 - ¾" x 8 ¾" rectangles *(from each)*
	C 3 - 1" x 8" rectangles *(from each)*
	D 3 - ¾" x 8" rectangles *(from each)*

Summer Moon Book by Carrie Nelson

Large Background
FRAMED BLOCK

Piecing Instructions:

Assemble Block using matching background fabric.

Large Background Framed Block should measure 8 ¾" x 8 ¾".

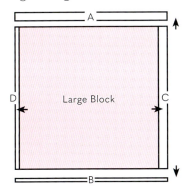
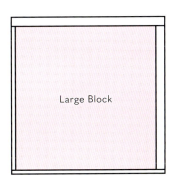

Make twenty-four Blocks.

Summer Moon Book by Carrie Nelson

Summer Moon Quilt
FINISHING

70 ½" x 78 ¾"

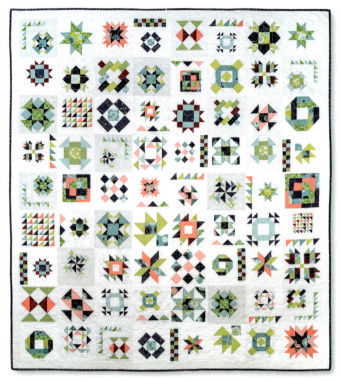

70 ½" x 78 ¾"

Vintage Fabric Requirements:

5085-11 Border ⅞ yard

5086-15 Binding ⅞ yard

5080-11 Backing 5 yards

Modern Fabric Requirements:

1685-11 Border ⅞ yard

1682-22M Binding ⅞ yard

1681-11M Backing 5 yards

Cutting Instructions:

		Complete Quilt
Border	A	9 - 2 ½" x width of fabric strips
Binding	B	9 - 2 ½" x width of fabric strips

Summer Moon Book by Carrie Nelson

Summer Moon Quilt
FINISHING

Quilt Center:
Assemble Quilt Center. Press rows in opposite directions.

Quilt Center should measure 66 ½" x 74 ¾".

Summer Moon Book by Carrie Nelson

Summer Moon Quilt
FINISHING

Border:

Piece the Fabric A strips end to end.

Subcut into:

    2 - 2 ½" x 74 ¾" strips (Side Borders - A1)

    2 - 2 ½" x 70 ½" strips (Top and Bottom Borders - A2)

Attach the Side Borders.

Attach the Top and Bottom Borders.

Binding:

Piece the Fabric B strips end to end for binding.

Quilt and bind as desired.

Summer Moon Quilt
FINISHING

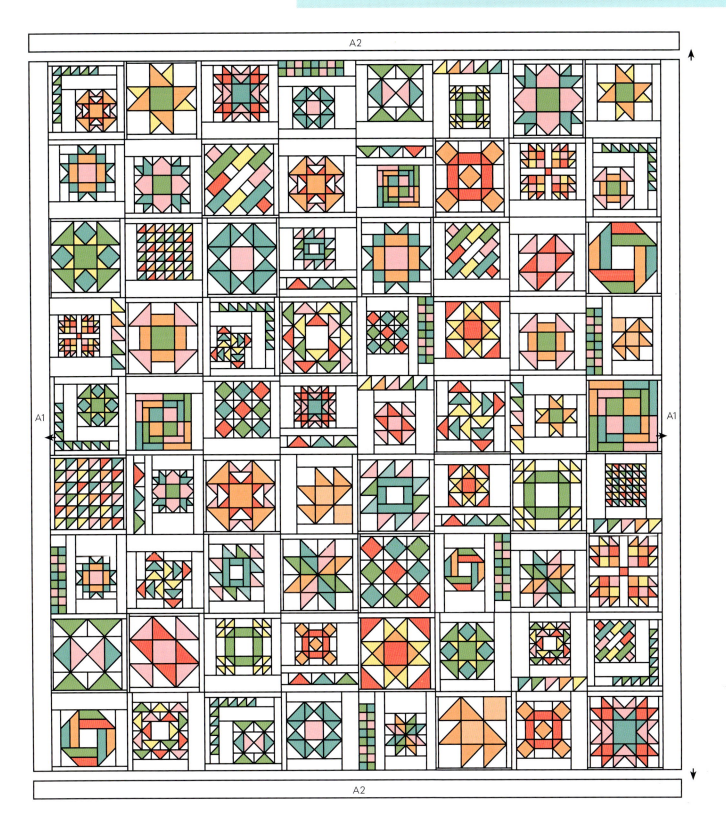

Summer Moon Book by Carrie Nelson

Summer Moon Book by Carrie Nelson